IMPLEMENTING STANDARDS-BASED EDUCATION

The Authors

Robert J. Marzano is a senior fellow at the Mid-continent Regional Educational Laboratory (McREL). He headed a team of authors to develop *Dimensions of Learning: Teacher's Manual*, published by the Association for Supervision and Curriculum Development (ASCD), and is senior author on *Tactics for Thinking* and *Literacy Plus: An Integrated Approach to Teaching Reading, Writing, Vocabulary, and Reasoning*. Most recently, his work has focused on standards and assessment. He and co-author John Kendall have written *A Comprehensive Guide to Designing Standards-Based Districts, Schools, and Classrooms* and *Content Knowledge: A Compendium of Standards and Benchmarks for K-12 Education*. His newest book is entitled *Transforming Classroom Grading and Assessment*.

John S. Kendall, a senior director at McREL in Aurora, Colorado, directs a technical assistance unit that provides standards-related services to schools, districts, and states, as well as to national and international organizations. He is the lead author of *Content Knowledge: A Compendium of Standards and Benchmarks for K-12 Education*. He and co-author Robert Marzano have written *A Comprehensive Guide to Designing Standards-Based Districts, Schools, and Classrooms* and a number of articles and book chapters related to standards and student assessment. He has also co-authored a number of articles and books on vocabulary and literacy.

Student Assessment Series

IMPLEMENTING STANDARDS-BASED EDUCATION

Robert J. Marzano and John S. Kendall

Glen W. Cutlip
Series Editor

NATIONAL EDUCATION ASSOCIATION

Note

The opinions expressed in this publication should not be construed as representing the policy or position of the National Education Association. These materials are intended to be discussion documents for educators who are concerned with specialized interests of the profession.

Reproduction of any part of this book must include the usual credit line and copyright notice. Address communications to Editor, NEA Teaching and Learning.

Library of Congress Cataloguing-in-Publication Data
Marzano, Robert J.
    Implementing standards-based education / Robert J. Marzano and John S. Kendall.
      p.   cm. — (Student assessment series)
    Includes bibliographical references (p.).
    ISBN 0-8106-2072-3
    1.   Education—Standards—United States.   2.   Educational tests and measurements—United States—Evaluation.   I. Kendall, John S.   II. National Education Association of the United States.   III. Title.   IV. Series.
    LB3060.83.M378 1998
    379.1'58'0973—dc21   98–43678
                                                     CIP

CONTENTS

INTRODUCTION

The field of student assessment—from methodology and techniques to the use of results—is changing, and these changes are dramatically affecting the work of education employees.

On one hand, these changes have created new options. For example, classroom assessment instruments have expanded to include assessments based on portfolios, projects, and performances. Teachers now assess a student's performance based on predetermined criteria more closely aligned with the instructional objectives of the lesson and tailor instruction more specifically to individual students. Students become partners with the teacher in assessment by having access to these criteria at the beginning of the lesson. Classroom assessment is truly becoming an integral part of the instructional program as more and more teachers add these assessment techniques to their repertoire.

On the other hand, changes in student assessment have created new concerns, especially in the use of assessment results. Today, assessment results are being used for more than comparing an individual student's performance against a state or national norm, and for more than providing data for making program improvement decisions. They are being used to determine the success or failure of teachers and schools. Policy makers and others are using large-scale assessments to decide whether teachers and schools are providing an adequate education to all students and attaching consequences, positive and negative, on the basis of student assessment results. The use of student test scores has raised the stakes for all education employees.

Consequently, student assessment is part of every teacher's work. In fact, nearly one-third of a classroom teacher's time is spent assessing and evaluating students. Many influential groups have identified competence in student assessment as essential for the training and licensing of new teachers and the upgrading of the skills of practicing teachers (National Board for Professional Teaching Standards, Interstate New Teacher Assessment Consortium, National Council for Accreditation of Teacher Education, Educational Testing Service, and the National Association of State Directors of Teacher Education and Certification). These groups estimate that less than one-half of currently practicing teachers have received adequate training in student assessment.

To help members and other educators keep abreast of the ever-changing field of student assessment, the National Education Association (NEA) commissioned leading assessment experts to write about student assessment from their perspectives. Experts Robert J. Marzano and John S. Kendall, the authors of this book on implementing standards-based education, propose two approaches for consideration and use. Both the direct and the indirect approaches to standards implementation are assessment based. The book is intended to be of use to teachers at all levels, preschool through graduate studies, as well as to other education employees.

The NEA developed the Student Assessment Series to help teachers and other education employees improve their knowledge and skills in student assessment and hopes readers will find the series a valuable resource for current and future student assessment practices.

Glen W. Cutlip
Series Editor

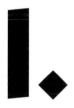

THE STANDARDS MOVEMENT

The purpose of this book is twofold: to help teachers understand the rationale and nature of the current emphasis in American education on standards, and to provide classroom teachers with guidance in the many ways the standards movement might affect their classrooms.

In writing this book, we have assumed that classroom teachers in America will inevitably be affected by the standards movement in the very near future. Virtually every state now has standards in core content areas or is in the process of generating those standards. More specifically, according to a 1997 report by the American Federation of Teachers (AFT) (see Gandal 1997), 49 states either have or are in the process of setting standards. The only state that is not setting standards at the state level is Iowa; yet Iowa educators are expected to establish content standards at the local district level. In short, every state in the nation is moving toward setting rigorous content standards.

What does this movement mean for the typical classroom teacher? How will it affect the way you do business in your classroom? Before addressing these questions, we begin with a brief history of the standards movement.

A Brief History of the Modern Standards Movement

Most educators trace the beginning of the modern standards movement to the publication of the highly visible and controversial 1983 report, *A Nation At Risk*. Researcher Lorrie Shepard (1993) notes that with the publication of this report, the rhetoric of educational reform changed dramatically to a concern for the very safety of our country. Who will soon forget the often quoted words from *A Nation At Risk*: "The educational foundations of our society are presently being eroded by a rising tide of mediocrity that threatens our very future as a nation and a people...We have, in effect, been committing an act of unthinking, unilateral, educational disarmament" (National Commission on Excellence in Education 1983, p. 5). Without doubt, the report engendered in American society a deep concern for the quality and future of American education.

The concern about the viability of our educational system eventually led President George Bush and the nation's governors to call an education summit in Charlottesville, Virginia, in September 1987. There, President Bush and the nation's governors agreed upon six broad goals published under the title *The National Education Goals Report: Building a Nation of Learners* (National Education Goals Panel [NEGP] 1991). Two of these goals (3 and 4) related specifically to academic standards:

Goal 3: By the year 2000, American students will leave grades four, eight, and twelve having demonstrated competency in challenging subject matter, including English, mathematics, science, history, and geography; and every school in America will ensure that all students learn to use their minds well, so they may be prepared for responsible citizenship, further learning, and productive employment in our modern economy.

Goal 4: By the year 2000, U.S. students will be first in the world in science and mathematics achievement. (p. 4)

The summit inspired intense activity on the part of national subject-matter organizations to establish standards in their respective content areas. These groups looked for guidance from the National Council of Teachers of Mathematics (NCTM), which published the *Curriculum and Evaluation Standards for School Mathematics* in 1989. To date, standards have been established in the vast majority of subject areas addressed in education. Many of the efforts to identify standards were funded by the U.S. Department of Education under the leadership of Secretary of Education Lamar Alexander.

The documents listed in Figure 1 are the results of efforts by groups that either were funded by the U.S. Department of Education or identify themselves as representing the national consensus in their subject areas.

Even though these documents were intended to constitute a de facto set of national standards, individual states soon began to develop their own standards documents. Exactly why individual states would elect to construct their own standards when "national" documents had been created is perplexing to some. Perhaps it is because of the assumption in this country that school policy and curricula should be set at the state level as opposed to the federal level. As Fred Temper, an associate superintendent in the California Department of Education explained: "I guess like most states we'd like to feel that we can set our own standards" (in Olson 1995a, p. 15).

State efforts to create standards were given an impressive endorsement at the second education summit, convened by President Bill Clinton, in Palisades, New York, in March 1996, when the state governors committed to designing state standards (National Governors Association 1996). These actions are consistent with the opinions of many educators and noneducators who believe that it is at the state level that the standards movement will either succeed or fail. As education reporter Lynn Olson (1995a) notes:

The U.S. Constitution makes it clear: States bear the responsibility for educating their citizens. They decide how long students continue their education and how the schools are financed. They control what is taught, what is tested, which textbooks are used, and how teachers are trained.

Thus, despite all the talk about national education standards, it is the 50 individual states that ultimately will determine what students should know and be able to do. (p. 15)

Although most states had either created standards or were close to completing their standards as of 1997, not all the state efforts have stood up well to a critical scrutiny. To illustrate, the 1997 report by the American Federation of Teachers (Gandal 1997) noted the following:

1. The commitment to standards-based reform remains very strong in the states.
2. Most states still need to improve some of their standards in order to provide the basis for a common core of learning.
3. States continue to have difficulty setting strong standards in English and social studies.

Although the standards movement is strong all across the nation, its impact has not yet dramatically affected the lives of classroom teachers. Some believe it is the very nature of the standards movement to be indirect in its influence. Researchers Robert Glaser and Robert Linn (1993) assert that it might be only in retrospect that we recognize the importance of the standards movement in American education.

In the recounting of our nation's drive toward educational reform, the last decade of this century will undoubtedly be identified as the time when a concentrated press for national education standards emerged. The press for standards was evidenced by the efforts of federal and state legislators, presidential and gubernatorial candidates, teacher and subject-matter specialists, councils, governmental agencies, and private foundations. (p. xiii)

We believe that some approaches to implementing standards-based reform will have direct impact on the culture of the classroom; whereas other approaches will have more indirect effects.

Two Approaches to Implementing Standards

As a result of our work with schools and districts across the country, we at the Mid-continent Regional Educational Laboratory (McREL) in Aurora, Colorado, have noticed that approaches to implementing standards may be organized into two general categories—indirect and direct. It is important to note that these categories describe the impact of standards on the day-to-day life of classroom teachers; they may have little reference to the impact on students. That is, an approach to implementing standards that has an *indirect* impact on the day-to-day life of the teacher in the classroom may have a *direct* impact on the lives of individual students.

Indirect approaches, as the name implies, do not mandate that teachers address standards in their classrooms. Rather, the assumption is that even though student performance on standards is not directly tied to their performance in individual classes,

Figure 1
"Official" Standards Documents

Subject Area	Organization and Document
Science	National Research Council. 1996. *National Science Education Standards.* Washington, D.C.: National Academy Press.
Foreign Language	National Standards in Foreign Language Education Project. 1996. *Standards for Foreign Language Learning: Preparing for the 21st Century.* Lawrence, Kans.: Allen Press, Inc.
English Language Arts	National Council of Teachers of English and the International Reading Association. 1996. *Standards for the English Language Arts.* Urbana, Ill.: National Council of Teachers of English.
History	National Center for History in the Schools. 1994. *National Standards for History for Grades K-4: Expanding Children's World in Time and Space.* Los Angeles: Author. National Center for History in the Schools. 1994. *National Standards for United States History: Exploring the American Experience.* Los Angeles: Author. National Center for History in the Schools. 1994. *National Standards for World History: Exploring Paths to the Present.* Los Angeles: Author. National Center for History in the Schools. 1996. *National Standards for History: Basic Edition.* Los Angeles: Author.
Arts	Consortium of National Arts Education Associations. 1994. *National Standards for Arts Education: What Every Young American Should Know and Be Able to Do in the Arts.* Reston, Va.: Music Educators National Conference.
Health	Joint Committee on National Health Education Standards. 1995. *National Health Education Standards: Achieving Health Literacy.* Reston, Va.: Association for the Advancement of Health Education.
Civics	Center for Civic Education. 1994. *National Standards for Civics and Government.* Calabasas, Ca.: Author.
Economics	National Council on Economic Education. August 1996. *Content Statements for State Standards in Economics, K-12* (Draft). New York: Author
Geography	Geography Education Standards Project. 1994. *Geography for Life: National Geography Standards.* Washington, D.C.: National Geographic Research and Exploration.

Figure 1 (continued)
"Official" Standards Documents

Subject Area	Organization and Document
Physical Education	National Association for Sport and Physical Education. 1995. *Moving into the Future, National Standards for Physical Education: A Guide to Content and Assessment.* St. Louis: Mosby.
Mathematics	National Council of Teachers of Mathematics. 1989. *Curriculum and Evaluation Standards for School Mathematics.* Reston, Va.: Author.
Social Studies	National Council for the Social Studies. 1994. *Expectations of Excellence: Curriculum Standards for Social Studies.* Washington, D.C.: Author.

teachers will quite naturally want to provide assistance to their students and organize classroom practice accordingly. Commonly, when indirect approaches are employed, individual teachers have the flexibility to pick and choose those standards they will address in their classrooms. In effect, the change in classroom practice is implicit in these approaches. As we shall see, indirect approaches are commonly attempts to address problems inherent in some school systems, such as a lack of relationships between what is taught and what is tested.

Direct approaches, as the name implies, necessitate a change in classroom practice for teachers. Additionally, the specific standards that must be addressed in a given class are mandated. Teachers cannot pick and choose those standards they will address. In Section II, we consider indirect approaches; in Section III we consider direct approaches.

II.

INDIRECT APPROACHES TO IMPLEMENTING STANDARDS

As described in Section I, indirect approaches do not mandate a change in classroom practice, but teachers commonly attend to standards in their classrooms as an aid to students. There are at least two specific approaches within this category: (1) external tests and (2) projects, exhibitions, and portfolios. Before discussing these two different types of indirect approaches, we should note that they can be viewed as attempts to solve some specific problems that plague American education. Among these are the lack of a well-articulated curriculum and an emphasis on educational "inputs" as opposed to educational "outputs." We consider the issue of curriculum first.

To the noneducator, it probably seems that public schools have a well-articulated curriculum. Most school district central offices can produce "curriculum guides" that specify in detail the topics that will be covered in every subject area and generally at every grade level. One would think, then, that the curriculum within any given school district is a well-honed system. Yet, when one probes into the curricular structure of schools, one generally finds that the perception of a well-articulated course of study from grade level to grade level is just that—a perception. E. D. Hirsch, outspoken critic of American education and author of the highly popular book *Cultural Literacy: What Every American Needs to Know* (Hirsch 1987), addresses this point in his latest book, *The Schools We Need: Why We Don't Have Them* (Hirsch 1997):

> We know, of course, that there exists no national curriculum, but we assume, quite reasonably, that agreement has been reached locally regarding what should be taught to children at each grade level—if not within the whole district, then certainly within an individual school. . . .But. . .the idea that there exists a coherent plan for teaching content within the local district, or even within the individual school, is a gravely misleading myth. (p. 26)

Hirsch goes on to explain that the myth of a coherent curriculum is not a darkly held secret. Rather, the notion that there is a local curriculum is simply assumed by most educators as a matter of faith. To illustrate, Hirsch relates the following anecdote:

> Recently, a district superintendent told me that for twenty years he had mistakenly assumed each of his schools was determining what would be taught to children at each grade level, but was shocked to find that assumption entirely false; he discovered that no principal in his district could tell him what minimal content each child in a grade was expected to learn. (pp. 26-27)

Although we do not agree with the solutions Hirsch proposes for the problems within K-12 education, we do believe he has a point. Research verifies that what is written in curriculum guides is not necessarily what happens in the classroom.

The lack of attention to the written curriculum has been demonstrated in a number of ways. Specifically, studies (Doyle 1992; Stodolsky 1989; Yoon, Burstein, and Gold n.d.) indicate that even when highly structured textbooks are used, teachers commonly make independent and idiosyncratic decisions regarding what should be emphasized, what should be added, and what should be deleted. To illustrate, in their book *The Learning Gap*, researchers Stevenson and Stigler (1992) make the following observations:

> Daunted by the length of most textbooks and knowing that the children's future teachers will be likely to return to the material, American teachers often omit some topics. Different topics are omitted by different teachers thereby making it impossible for the children's later teachers to know what has been covered at earlier grades—they cannot be sure what their students know and do not know. (p. 140)

The lack of uniformity in American curriculum is also evident in the research on how teachers use time. To illustrate, in a study of the content that teachers emphasize within reading and the language arts, researcher David Berliner (1979, 1984) found that one fifth-grade teacher allocated 68 minutes a day of instruction in reading and language arts; another teacher allotted 137 minutes a day. At the second-grade level, one teacher set aside 47 minutes a day for reading and language arts; another teacher set aside 118 minutes a day, or $2\frac{1}{2}$ times more per day, to teach reading and language arts. Researcher Charles Fisher and his colleagues (Fisher et al.1980) reported the following anecdotes and commentary on variation in the curriculum:

> In one second-grade class the average student received 9 minutes of instruction over the whole school year in the arithmetic associated with the use of money. This figure can be contrasted with classes where the average second grader was allocated 315 minutes per school year in the curriculum

content area of money. As another example, in the fifth grade some classes received less than 1,000 minutes of instruction in reading comprehension for the school year (about 10 minutes per day). This figure can be contrasted with classes where the average student was allocated almost 5,000 minutes of instruction related to comprehension during the school year (about 50 minutes per day).

The differences in time allocations at the level of "reading" and "mathematics" and at the level of specific subcontent areas are substantial. These differences in how teachers allocate time are related to differences in student learning. Other things being equal, the more time allocated to a content area, the higher the academic achievement. (p. 16)

In short, in practice, American school systems do not appear to have a clear delineation of what should be addressed at each grade level. The intent behind indirect approaches to implementing standards is that they will compel teachers to focus on specific content at specific grade levels. For example, if all students must "pass" a standards-based test at a particular grade level, teachers will most probably want to emphasize the content on that test. A comprehensive, standards test with high stakes attached to it will indirectly drive the curriculum—so goes the logic.

Another problem the indirect approaches are designed to address is the traditional emphasis in public education on "inputs" as opposed to "outputs." This issue was addressed by former Assistant Secretary of Education Chester Finn. Finn (1990) describes this shift in perspective in terms of an emerging paradigm for education:

Under the *old* conception (dare I say paradigm?), education was thought of as process and system, effort and intention, investment and hope. To improve education meant to try harder, to engage in more activity, to magnify one's plans, to give people more services, and to become more efficient in delivering them.

Under the *new* definition, now struggling to be born, education is the result achieved, the learning that takes root when the process has been effective. *Only* if the process succeeds and learning occurs will we say that *education* happened. Absent evidence of such a result, there is no education—however, many attempts have been made, resources deployed, or energies expended. (p. 586)

Finn explained that the inherent shortcomings of the old "input" paradigm of schooling became apparent in the mid-1960s when the U.S. Office of Education was commissioned by Congress to conduct a study of the quality of American education. Researcher James Coleman was the chief author of the resulting report, the celebrated "Coleman Report" released in 1966. Coleman summarized the importance of his study in the following way:

The major virtue of the study as conceived and executed lay in the fact that it did not accept the [traditional] definition, and by refusing to do so, has had its major impact in shifting policy attention from its traditional focus on comparison of inputs (the traditional measures of school quality used by school administrators: per-pupil expenditures, class size, teacher salaries, age of building and equipment, and so on) to a focus on output, and the effectiveness of inputs for bringing about changes in output. (1972, pp. 149-150)

Finn explained that the report did irrevocable damage to the old "input" paradigm and began the emphasis on educational outputs. Of course, the output characteristic that is the most salient to the majority of the people is student achievement—hence, the connection to the indirect approaches to standards implementation. Implementing standards by requiring students to take a test or complete a project establishes a very concrete output variable (i.e., the test or the project).

We might say, then, that indirect approaches are attempts to correct some inherent problems with the manner in which American education is conducted. The first type of indirect approach we consider is external tests.

External Tests

When a school or district adopts the external test approach to implementing standards, it utilizes the score or scores on specific tests as the sole or primary indicator of whether students have acquired certain knowledge. Use of a test as the primary way of implementing standards is commonly the first, and sometimes only, approach considered by state departments of education. This is evidenced by President Clinton's comments on March 27, 1996, when speaking to the National Governors Association at the Second Education Summit:

I believe every state, if you're going to have meaningful standards, must require a test for children to move, let's say, from elementary to middle school, or from middle school to high school, or to have a full-meaning high school diploma. And I don't think they should measure just minimum competency. You should measure what you expect these standards to measure. (pp. 6-7)

It is useful to think of traditional tests falling into two structural categories and three functional categories. The structural categories are *norm-referenced tests (NRTs)* and *criterion-referenced tests (CRTs)*. NRTs compare student test performance against that of other students—usually a national sample—and generally report student performance as a percentile score. CRTs compare students to an agreed upon "cut-score"—the minimum percentage students must answer correctly to receive a passing score. To illustrate, if a student does not receive a specific minimum score on the mathematics subtest on a CRT, he or she will be assessed as not having met the criterion—the cut-score—for that subtest. Both NRTs and CRTs rely heavily on multiple-choice items.

To implement standards, CRTs are almost always the type of test used. The reason is fairly straightforward. CRTs provide a pass/fail decision about students that is quite consistent with the concept of "meeting a standard" within the standards movement.

The functional categories for tests are *off-the-shelf tests*, *state-mandated tests*, and *district-designed tests*. As their name implies, off-the-shelf tests are those that a school or district purchases from a testing company. They are referred to as "off-the-shelf" because they can be purchased as one would purchase an item off the shelf of a store (Bond, Friedman, and van der Ploeg 1994). A number of leading companies produce and publish off-the-shelf tests. Among the most widely used are:

California Achievement Tests
Comprehensive Test of Basic Skills
Iowa Test of Basic Skills
Metropolitan Achievement Tests
Sequential Tests of Educational Progress
SRA Achievement Series
Stanford Achievement Tests (Cannell 1988)

Many of these tests can be interpreted in a norm-referenced fashion or a criterion-referenced fashion.

The second functional category of tests is state-mandated tests. According to measurement expert Peter Airasian (1994), state-mandated tests have been common in the United States since the mid-1980s. He notes that "The aim of these tests is to centralize educational decision making at the state level and to prod teachers and pupils to work harder to pass the tests" (p. 369).

Certainly, state-level tests appear to be the preferred testing approach within the standards movement. However, state-level standards tests have come under some harsh criticism of late. To illustrate, in a 1997 study of state assessment systems reported in a document entitled *Testing Our Children: A Report Card on State Assessment Systems*, researcher Monty Neill made the following observations:

- Even though almost every state has content standards, many state tests are not based on their standards and many important areas in their standards are not assessed.
- Most states rely far too heavily on multiple-choice testing and fail to provide an adequate range of methods for students to demonstrate their learning.
- States are generally weak in providing adequate performance development in interpreting and utilizing the results of state assessments. (Neill 1997, pp. 5-6)

The report noted that, in all, only seven states had assessment systems that did not need at least some significant improvements. These states were Colorado, Connecticut, Kentucky, Maine, Missouri, New Hampshire, and Vermont. All other state assessment systems were judged to need significant improvement, with 15 states needing "a complete overhaul" of their assessment systems (Neill 1997, p. 7).

The vast majority of states have assessments. As yet, however, not all require students to obtain a specific score for high school graduation, although the legislative rhetoric in most states would lead one to believe otherwise. Specifically, as reported by Neill (1997), 17 states currently require students to obtain a specific score on a specific test in order to graduate from high school. Two states require a test for graduation, but will allow districts to identify acceptable alternatives. Four states plan to have a test in place as of 1997. Finally, two states have a graduation test, but they do not require students to obtain a specific score for graduation. In all, then, 22 states either have, or plan to have soon, some form of test that students must pass for high school graduation. This information is summarized in Figure 2.

The third functional category is district-designed tests. McMillan (1997) warns that individual districts rarely have the technical expertise to develop their own tests. Many test publishers, however, are able to customize reports for individual districts. "These reports indicate specific skills and may include standards that are set by the state or district" (p. 88). In practice, then, district-designed tests are commonly customized, off-the-shelf tests.

Weaknesses of External Tests

Although external tests certainly have a role to play in the implementation of standards, they have some inherent weaknesses that educators should be aware of. According to Neill, many of the tests students must pass for high school graduation rely heavily on traditional types of items such as multiple-choice items. Neill explains:

> Unfortunately, most states rely too heavily on multiple-choice items and fail to use a reasonable range of assessment methods. Excluding writing assessments, of the 50 states, 26 rely entirely or nearly entirely on multiple-choice. Another 16-18 rely mostly on multiple-choice (have less than half their scores derived from constructed-response items; in two states, the proportions were not clear, but appear to be around the one-half point). Only 6-8 states have less than half multiple-choice items. (1997, p. 15)

The problem with an over-reliance on multiple-choice items is that they characteristically measure a narrow range of skills only. In fact, some studies have found that they do not address students' abilities to apply knowledge or think critically about knowledge (see Marzano 1990; Marzano and Costa 1988). Assessment expert Ruth Mitchell (1992) chronicles the many weaknesses of standardized tests:

> No matter how sophisticated the techniques, however, multiple-choice tests corrupt the teaching and learning process for the following reasons:
> 1. Even at their best, multiple-choice tests ask students to select a response. Selection is passive; it asks students to recognize, not to construct, an answer. The students do not contribute their own thinking to the answer.
> 2. Multiple-choice tests promote the false impression that a right or wrong answer is available for all questions and problems. As we know, few situations in life have a correct or incorrect answer.

Figure 2
State High School Graduation Tests

State	1	2	3	4	State	1	2	3	4
AL	X				MT				
AK		X			NC	X			
AR		X			ND				
AZ		X			NE				
CA					NH				
CO					NJ	X			
CT					NM	X			
DE		X	X		NV	X			
FL	X				NY	X			
GA	X				OH	X			
HI	X				OK				
IA					OR				
ID					PA				
IL					RI				
IN			X		SC	X			
KS					SD				
KY					TN	X			
LA	X				TX	X			
MA			X		UT				
MD	X				VA	X			
ME					VT				
MI				X	WA				
MN		X			WI			X	
MO					WV				X
MS	X				WY				

1 = State has a high school graduation test.
2 = State has a high school graduation test, but will accept an alternative.
3 = State plans to have a high school graduation test.
4 = State has a high school test, but it is not required for a diploma.

Source: Adapted from Monty Neill and others, *Testing Our Children: A Report Card on State Assessment Systems* (Cambridge, Mass.: National Center for Fair and Open Testing [Fairtest], 1997).

3. The tests tend to rely on memorization and the recall of facts or algorithms. They do not allow students to demonstrate understanding of how algorithms work.
4. The form of multiple-choice tests means that test makers select what can easily be tested rather than what is important for students to learn.
5. Multiple-choice tests do not accurately record what students know and can do, either positively or negatively, as a personal example shows. In 1974, I passed by four points over the cut score the German-language examination to qualify for the Ph.D., and I am on record somewhere as having a reading knowledge of German. But I cannot read any word of German that does not look like an English or Latin cognate. My answers were either guesses or choices based on probabilities. If the graduate examiners had really wanted to know if I could read German, I should have been required to translate a passage.
6. The tests trivialize teaching and learning. If all classroom activity— the books, the lectures, the discussions, the exercises, the home-work—ends up in a few bubbles taking no more than an hour, then what is all the fuss about? The end is incommensurate with the means. Students know that much of passing multiple-choice tests is test wisdom—how to guess productively, what items to omit—and they invest only enough effort to get by. (pp. 15-16)

Countering the Weaknesses of External Tests

To offset the weaknesses of tests that rely on multiple-choice items, many state assessment systems are including the use of performance tasks. Performance tasks require students to construct their responses rather than select from a list of options as do multiple-choice. (We will consider performance tasks in depth in a subsequent section.) For this reason, performance tasks are commonly referred to as "con-structed-response" items. To illustrate, consider the following mathematics task designed by the National Assessment of Educational Progress (NAEP 1992) and administered to a representative sample of eighth graders across the country:

> Treena won a 7-day scholarship worth $1,000 to the Pro Shot Basketball Camp. Round-trip travel expenses to the camp are $335 by air or $125 by train. At the camp she must choose between a week of individual instruc-tion at $60 per day or a week of group instruction at $40 per day. Treena's food and other expenses are fixed at $45 per day. If she does not plan to spend any money other than the scholarship, what are all choices of travel and instruction plans that she could afford to make? Explain your reason-ing. (Dossey, Mullis, and Jones 1993, p. 116)

As described by researchers John Dossey, Ina Mullis, and Chancey Jones (1993), this task requires the following types of thinking and reasoning:

The solution to this task requires students to use everyday consumer sense to determine Treena's fixed expenses and analyze the various choices she has for travel (plane or train) and instruction (individual or group). Students also must compare the total cost for each of the four alternatives to which this analysis leads to the $1,000 value of Treena's scholarship, in order to conclude which choices meet the given conditions. (p. 116)

One of the most powerful aspects of performance tasks is that they commonly require students to explain their reasoning. This allows for a glimpse into the systems of logic employed by students—information not accessible with the multiple-choice format. This trait has spawned a veritable flood of support for their use as supplements to standardized tests or as alternatives to standardized tests (see Archbald and Newmann 1988; Baron 1991; Baron and Kallick 1985; Berk 1986a, 1986b; Frederiksen and Collins 1989; Marzano 1990; Marzano and Costa 1988; Mitchell 1992; Resnick 1987a, 1987b; Resnick and Resnick 1992; Shepard 1989; Stiggins 1994; Wiggins 1989, 1991, 1993a, 1993b; Winograd and Perkins 1996).

Knowing the Exact Content of the Test

Regardless of whether an external test uses multiple-choice items, performance tasks, or both, or is developed by a national publishing company, the local state department, or the district, it behooves the classroom teacher to know the exact content covered in the test and make sure that its content is covered as a normal part of classroom work. Stated differently, an external test indirectly affects the classroom teacher in that it creates a responsibility for him or her to cover certain content. Unfortunately, this approach violates a misguided principle held by many educators that might be stated as follows: "It is unethical to teach to a test." In fact, one of the basic tenets of the modern standards movement is that teachers should teach to tests (Wiggins 1989). Where, then, did educators get the impression that it is unethical to teach to a test?

Researcher Grant Wiggins explains that the prohibition against teaching to a test springs from an inaccurate assumption that secrecy is a fundamental aspect of effective assessment. In his book, *Assessing Student Performance: Exploring the Purpose and Limits of Testing* (1993b), Wiggins notes that "This assumption is so common that we barely give it a second thought; the tests that we and others design to evaluate the success of student learning invariably depend upon secrecy" (p. 72).

The assumption that tests should be kept secret from those who must take them is fallacious from at least two perspectives. First, it violates a basic right individuals have to know the criteria on which they are being judged, particularly if the judgments are to have high-stakes implications for students. Wiggins defends this right of students to receive prior information regarding what they will be tested on and how they will be tested.

Why would we take for granted that students do not have a right to full knowledge and justification of the form and content of each test and the standards by which their work will be judged? The student's (and often the teacher's) future is at stake, yet neither has an opportunity to question the aptness or adequacy of the test, the keying of the answers, or the scoring of the answers. Why would we assume that any test designer—be it a company or a classroom teacher—has a prior right to keep such information from test takers (and often test users)? Why would we assume, contrary to all accepted guidelines of experimental research, that test companies (and teachers) need not publish their tests and results after the fact for scrutiny by independent experts as well as the test taker? Maybe the better advice to test makers is that offered twenty years ago by performance assessment researchers Robert Fitzpatrick and Edward Morrison: "The best solution to the problem of test security is to keep no secrets." (p. 73)

The assumption that test content should be kept secret is fallacious also because it makes sense only if one assumes that a test can be designed in such a way that it adequately represents a student's competence in the subject matter that is tested. In other words, it makes sense to keep a test secret if individuals who are competent in the subject matter being tested will invariably receive high scores on the test and individuals who are not competent in the subject matter will invariably receive low scores. If this were true, test secrecy might be considered fair since students would do well on a subject-matter test as long as they had mastered the subject matter tested. Unfortunately, current research has shown that this is a rarely the case.

Generalizability of One Test Score

In the last two decades, a relatively new area of measurement theory has been applied to educational testing. This new area is referred to as "generalizability theory." Although it is quite complex in practice, generalizability theory is used to determine how generalizable a student's score on one test is to his or her performance on another test of the same subject matter (Brennan 1983; Feldt and Brennan 1993). Research has shown that a student might receive a high score on subject matter tested one way, but a low score when the same subject matter is tested a different way. In a series of studies (Shavelson and Baxter 1992; Shavelson, Gao, and Baxter 1993; Shavelson and Webb 1991; Shavelson, Webb, and Rowley 1989), researcher Richard Shavelson and his colleagues gave students the same science task in three different formats (hands-on, computer-simulated, and written descriptions derived from a hands-on experiment). They found that while a student might perform well in one format, he or she might perform badly in the other two. It is important to note that Shavelson's research was conducted on performance tasks as opposed to multiple-choice items. Such findings have led Shavelson and his colleagues to conclude that a single performance assessment is not a good general indicator of how well students can perform within a content area. In fact, measurement experts (e.g., Lane, Liu, Ankenmann, and Stone 1996; Linn 1994; Shavelson, Gao, and Baxter 1993) now contend that anywhere from 10 to 36 performance tasks are necessary to assess accurately students' competence within a single subject area. In short, an individual's score on a single performance task is not a generalizable indicator of the individual's competence in the subject matter assessed by the performance task.

The lack of generalizability of performance tasks creates the possibility that a student might perform poorly on a specific task, but, in fact, be competent in the knowledge and skills the task is supposed to assess. For example, consider the following story that appeared in *The Wall Street Journal* about a high school senior who had taken a performance task designed by the local state department of education:

> Jonathan, 17 years old, was declared a novice at writing. But by that time, he had already been accepted at the Massachusetts Institute of Technology, California Institute of Technology, Carnegie Mellon University, Rensselaer Polytechnic Institute and the University of Illinois. He had earned a perfect score on the American College Testing, or ACT, exam, which Mid-western states favor over the Scholastic Aptitude Test; he had scored a near-perfect 770 out of 800 on the verbal portion of the SAT; he had accumulated a 3.993 grade point average: he was a National Merit Scholar, had a perfect grade in advance-placement English, and was on his way to graduating at the head of his class. (March 1997)

Tests that are composed of multiple-choice items also run the risk of not being generalizable. This is particularly the case if fewer than six items are used to assess a particular topic (see Linn and Gronlund 1995, p. 442). Unfortunately, an examination of tests that use multiple-choice items shows that many topics are assessed with relatively few items. To illustrate, Figure 3 provides an analysis of the number of items used to assess various topics in a commonly used standardized test.

As Figure 3 illustrates, the number of items used to assess a given topic ranges from 3 to 11. One might legitimately ask if a student's score on subtests designed to measure knowledge of health and safety with 3 items is a generalizable indicator of his or her knowledge of that topic. Probably not. It should also be noted that the particular test from which the item count in Figure 3 was derived is one of the most commonly used standardized tests on the market. There is nothing wrong with this particular test. It is a simple fact that it is very difficult to design a single test that is a generalizable measure of competence within a domain.

The research on generalizability clearly indicates that tests designed outside the classroom to assess large numbers of students on their competence in specific standards commonly address very specific information. This means that unless classroom teachers are keenly aware of the content and format of the items on these tests and address these items in their classrooms, they run the risk of their students receiving low scores on tests intended to cover content they know quite well. To aid classroom teachers, some testing companies provide fairly detailed descriptions of the content covered in their subtests. To illustrate, the publishing company Harcourt, Brace will supply information, upon request, about the content of the Stanford Achievement Tests. They report, for example, that their intermediate levels address

Figure 3

Analysis of Items on a Standardized Test

Content Area	Subtest	Number of Items
Word Analysis	Initial Sounds: words	5
	Letter Substitutions	5
	Word Building: vowels	5
	Vowel Sounds	11
	Silent Letters	3
	Affixes	3
Math Concepts	Number Systems	4
	Whole Numbers	3
	Geometry	5
	Measurement	6
	Fractions and Money	4
	Number Sentences	6
	Estimation	3
Social Studies	History	4
	Geography	6
	Economics	8
	Political Science	6
	Sociology and Anthropology	7
Science	Nature of Science	9
	Life Science	6
	Earth and Space	5
	Physical Science	8
	Health and Safety	3

the following topics in mathematics computation:
- addition with whole numbers
- subtraction with whole numbers
- multiplication with whole numbers

- division with whole numbers
- computation with fractions and decimals
- estimates.

Unfortunately, the publishers do not provide as much detail with regard to the content addressed in other areas such as science and the social sciences. (For a detailed discussion of the Stanford Achievement Tests, see Airasian 1994.) Similarly, the Riverside Publishing Company provides the following information about the content covered in the subtest on sources of information within the Iowa Test of Basic Skills, Level 8:

- locating specific places on maps
- determining directions on maps
- determining distances on maps.

They do not, however, provide as much detail relative to some of their other subtests, such as social studies. (For a detailed discussion of the Iowa Test of Basic Skills, see McMillan 1997.)

In short, if a teacher is willing to request the appropriate information, he or she can receive specific guidance relative to the content addressed in tests designed by some publishing companies. As yet this does not seem to be true for tests designed by state departments of education. As of the writing of this book, we have had little success in obtaining specific guidance relative to the content addressed in tests designed by state departments even though those state departments have contracted with national testing companies to develop their tests. In fairness, however, the failure of our efforts might very possibly be due to the fact that we have sampled only a few of the many states that have tests. Additionally, the states we did sample were in the process of designing their tests and, consequently, might not have been ready to release such information. In any event, state departments and districts that have designed their own standards tests should make public the specific content their tests address. Consequently, we urge classroom teachers who labor under the external test approach to contact the agencies that have designed those tests and press for detailed information about the content addressed in those tests.

Performance Tasks and Portfolios

The second approach to implementing standards that indirectly affects classroom teachers utilizes performance tasks and portfolios *constructed over time* as the primary measure of students' competence in standards. Many teachers use the terms *performance task* and *authentic task* synonymously, whereas some educators assert that the two are different. Evaluation specialist Carol Meyer (1992) explains that performance assessments involve situations in which students must construct responses that illustrate that they can apply knowledge. Authentic assessments also involve situations in which students must construct responses that demonstrate an application of knowledge. In authentic assessment, however, the situation is more "real life." Researchers Fred Newmann, Walter Secado, and Gary Wehlage (1995, 24-25) offer these examples of authentic tasks in geometry and social studies:

Authentic Geometric Task

Design packaging that will hold 576 cans of Campbell's Tomato Soup (net weight, $10\frac{1}{4}$ oz.) or packaging that will hold 144 boxes of Kellogg's Rice Krispies (net weight, 19 oz.). Use and list each individual package's real measurements; create scale drawings of front, top, and side perspectives; show the unfolded boxes/containers in a scale drawing; build a proportional, three-dimensional model.

Authentic Social Studies Task

Write a letter to a student living in South Central Los Angeles conveying your feeling about what happened in that area following the acquittal of police officers in the Rodney King case. Discuss the tension between our natural impulse to strike back at social injustice and the principles of nonviolence.

In fact, the line between an authentic task and a performance task is a fuzzy one. Is the mathematics task previously cited about Treena's trip to the Pro Shot Basketball Camp a performance task or is it an authentic task? Is it something that students might do in the real world? Does the task in which students design packages that hold differing quantities of various products represent a real-world problem? In the final analysis, we have concluded that performance tasks and authentic tasks are so similar in actual practice that the distinction is negligible. Consequently, we use the term *performance task* to refer to any task in which students are asked to apply their knowledge and defend their reasoning regardless of whether the task is one they might undertake in "real life."

One of the most interesting aspects of performance tasks is that with practice, students' abilities to do them can increase dramatically. To illustrate, in studies conducted at McREL, we have found that students' abilities to do performance tasks can be increased if teachers systematically use these tasks in the classroom. For example, in one elementary school, we gave performance tasks in mathematics to all children in first through fifth grades in September. Two skills were assessed in each performance task: the ability to problem-solve and the ability to communicate mathematically. The initial percentage of students providing a satisfactory or better than satisfactory score for these skills is reported in columns A and C of Figure 4.

In all, 16.6 percent of the students constructed satisfactory or better responses in the problem-solving component of the tasks and 15.6 percent in the communication component of the tasks given in September. The teachers who participated in the study considered these results unacceptable. All teachers desired higher percentages of students to receive satisfactory scores. During the year, classroom teachers presented students with performance tasks of their own design and at their own pace. As teachers interacted with students, they concentrated on asking them to explain what they did and why they did it.

At the end of the year, all students were given another performance task, which again was scored for problem-solving and communication. These posttest results are reported in columns B and D in Figure 4. The gains were dramatic: The percentage of students who achieved satisfactory or better responses in problem-solving rose to 65.6 percent (from 16.6%). Similarly, the percentage of students who achieved a satisfactory or better rating in communicating mathematically rose to 46.7 percent (from 15.6%). Even more impressive were the gains in the performance of African American and Hispanic students. For example, the percentage of African American students receiving a satisfactory or better score on problem solving rose from 8.5 percent to 50.8 percent. These results imply that if teachers systematically focus on performance tasks in the classroom, students' performance scores will increase.

It is important to note here that we are not advocating that teachers drill students on the exact performance task they will receive as part of a standards test, whether that test be assigned at the national, state, or district level. Rather, we are suggesting that students be provided with practice in performing types of tasks similar to the ones they might find on an external standards test. In effect, then, students receive practice in the general skills that cut across all performance tasks—not the specific content of any one task. We discuss the general skills in depth later in this section (see "Performance Tasks, Portfolios, and the Classroom Teacher").

Portfolios and performance tasks have a symbiotic relationship in that a portfolio is commonly a collection of performance tasks. Researchers Lauren Resnick and Daniel Resnick (1992) define portfolio assessment in the following way:

> A variant of the performance assessment is the *portfolio assessment*. In this method, frequently used in the visual and performing arts and other design fields, individuals collect their work over a period of time, select a sample of the collection that they think best represents their capabilities, and submit this portfolio of work to a jury or panel of judges. (p. 61)

Researcher Mark Reckase (1995) describes a portfolio as "a purposeful collection of student work that exhibits to the student (and/or others) the student's efforts, progress, or achievement in (a) given area(s)." (p. 21)

By their very nature, portfolios are oriented to subject areas that naturally involve products such as writing and the arts. Recently, there have been efforts to articulate the recommended contents of portfolios in subject areas that are not necessarily product-oriented. For example, mathematics teacher Pam Knight (1992) delineates a number of items that a mathematics portfolio should contain, including the following:

- samples of word problems in various stages of development along with the student's description of his or her thinking during the various problem–solving stages
- the student's self-evaluation of his or her understanding of the mathematical concepts that have been covered in class, along with examples
- the student's self-evaluation of his or her competence in the mathematical procedures, strategies, and algorithms that have been covered in class, along with examples.

When a district combines performance tasks and portfolios to form the primary indicators of students' performance on standards, it requires students to complete a

Figure 4
Pretest and Posttest Results on Performance Tasks

Ethnicity	A Pretest Problem Solving	B Posttest Problem Solving	C Pretest Communication	D Posttest Communication
Asian (25)	16.0% (4)	68.0% (17)	12.0% (3)	44.0% (11)
African American (130)	8.5% (11)	50.8% (66)	12.3% (16)	32.3% (42)
Hispanic (31)	3.2% (1)	77.4% (24)	0% (0)	48.4% (15)
White (116)	29.3% (34)	78.4% (24)	24.1% (28)	62.9% (73)
Grand Total (302)	16.6%	65.6%	15.6%	46.7%

Marzano, R.J., and J.S. Kendall, unpublished data. © 1992. Reprinted with permission of Mid-continent Regional Education Laboratory, Aurora, Colorado.

series of performance tasks that are organized into a portfolio. A useful comparison may be made between this approach and the first approach—external tests. Using the first approach, students must "pass" some type of external assessment to matriculate from one level to the next. In this sense, the external test and the performance task and portfolio are similar: both utilize some form of "exit assessment" to pass students on to the next level. As we have seen, both might even involve the use of performance tasks. Within the external tests approach, however, the exit assessments occur at a specific point in time. In effect, students take a test to pass from one level to the next. Even though that test may include or be totally composed of performance tasks, it is, nevertheless, a test administered within a relatively short interval at a specific point in time (e.g., a couple of hours on a specific day or week devoted to the administration of external tests). The difference between this approach and the performance task and portfolio approach is that the latter occurs over an extended period. In fact, students commonly work on their performance tasks and portfolios for months or even years before they actually perform their exhibitions.

The performance task and portfolio approach is perhaps the most popular model in current use. Indeed, much of the literature on standards-based education assumes the use of this approach. For example, researcher Joseph McDonald and his colleagues (McDonald, Smith, Turner, Finney, and Barton 1993) highlight this approach in their discussion of the innovations engendered through Theodore Sizer's Coalition of Essential Schools. The Coalition grew out of the studies that Sizer and his colleagues conducted between 1979 and 1984 (Sizer 1985; Powell, Farrar, and Cohen 1985; Hampel 1986). One of the key aspects of the Coalition philosophy is that diplomas should be awarded only after students have demonstrated their competence. In most Coalition schools, this principle manifests as an emphasis on performance tasks and portfolios.

One of the most frequently cited examples of the performance task and portfolio approach is Central Park East Secondary School (CPESS). According to researchers Linda Darling-Hammond and Jacqueline Ancess (1994), this school serves about 500 students, grades 7-12 in East Harlem. About 85 percent of its students are from Latino and African-American families, 60 percent qualify for free or reduced-price lunch, and 25 percent are eligible for special education services. The core of the CPESS approach is the completion of the following 14 projects organized into a portfolio:

1. A postgraduate plan
2. An autobiography
3. A report on school/community internship
4. A demonstration of an awareness of ethics and social issues
5. A demonstration of an appreciation of fine arts and ethics
6. A demonstration of an awareness of mass media
7. A demonstration of the importance and utility of "practical" skill areas such as medical care, independent living, legal rights, and securing a driver's license
8. A demonstration of an understanding of geography

9. A demonstration of competence to work in a language other than English, as a speaker, listener, reader, or writer
10. A demonstration of facility with the scientific method
11. A demonstration of competence in mathematics
12. A demonstration of an understanding and appreciation of a broad array of literature
13. A demonstration of an understanding of history and how it affects our lives today
14. A demonstration of participation in any team or as an individual, in a competitive or noncompetitive sport or activity. (pp. 14-15)

Darling-Hammond and Ancess explain that there is no one way to complete these projects or present them. A student might use a single performance task to fulfill a number of the 14 topics described above. To illustrate, Darling-Hammond and Ancess provide an account of how one student (Marlena) addressed the 14 required topics. She constructed one portfolio for three different internships in science that she took over a two-year period at Brookhaven National Laboratory, Hunter College, and Columbia University. She constructed another portfolio for mathematics that included mathematical models of rainfall developed under differing assumptions. Another portfolio was designed around her media project. It contained a sophisticated, evidence-based analysis of race, gender, and class stereotyping in prime-time television. Her history portfolio traced the history of segregated education in the United States and applied it to current debates about Afrocentric schools. This project was also used as Marlena's entry for ethics and social issues (see number 4 above).

Teachers at CPESS evaluate each portfolio on a 20-point grid scoring system. This numeric scale is then translated to a more qualitative descriptive scale: distinguished (18-20), satisfactory (15-17), and minimally satisfactory (12-14). Below a score of twelve, students must resubmit their projects.

Scores on the projects are recorded in a special section of the transcripts. Figure 5 depicts the portfolio section of Marlena's transcripts.

Performance Tasks, Portfolios, and the Classroom Teacher

When a school or district uses performance tasks and portfolios as the method of implementing standards, it usually allows for a good deal of student choice relative to the specific subject content that will be addressed. Recall that CPESS specifies general topics only in its list of 14 elements in which students must demonstrate competence. Consequently, the job of the classroom teacher is to provide guidance and coaching for students as they design their performance tasks. For example, a teacher interacting with Marlena from CPESS might have helped her identify the specific geography content (see number 8) on which Marlena wished to focus her investigation, the types and specific works of literature (see number 12) Marlena wished to analyze, and so on. The teacher, then, is not so much a provider of content as a resource and guide to students within the performance task and portfolio approach.

In addition, the teacher has the responsibility of teaching and reinforcing three general skill areas commonly found in most performance tasks. These are illustrated in the following performance task designed to be used in a history class:

For the next two weeks we will be studying American military conflicts of the past three decades, in particular the Vietnam War. You will form teams of two and pretend that you and your partner will be featured in a newsmagazine television special about military conflict. Your team has been asked to help viewers understand the basic elements of the Vietnam War by relating them to a situation that has nothing to do with military conflict but has the same basic elements. You are free to choose any nonmilitary situation you wish. In your explanation, the two of you must describe how the nonmilitary conflict fits each of the basic elements you identified in the war. You will prepare a report, with appropriate visuals, to present to the class in the way you would actually present it if you were doing your feature on the newsmagazine special. You will be assessed on and provided rubrics for the following:

1. your understanding of the specific details of the Vietnam War
2. your ability to identify the similarities and differences between the Vietnam War and the nonmilitary conflict you selected
3. your ability to design and deliver a report
4. your ability to work as an effective member of a team.

As the directions to the students reveal, this task is designed to measure four areas. Only the first area deals with history content per se. The remaining three address areas almost always embedded in a performance task: (1) thinking and reasoning, (2) communication, and (3) lifelong learning. These are the general skills commonly embedded in all performance tasks. Consequently, providing students with practice in these skills can enhance their performance on many, if not most, of the performance tasks they encounter.

Thinking and Reasoning. Over 80 years ago, education philosopher John Dewey (1916) wrote, "The sole direct path to enduring improvement in the methods of instruction and learning consists in centering upon the conditions which exact, promote, and test thinking" (p. 6). More recently, calls for the enhancement of thinking and reasoning in American education have come from the National Science Board Commission on Precollege Education in Mathematics, Science and Technology (1983), the College Board (1983), and the National Education Association (Futrell 1987). Additionally, the need to enhance students' abilities to think and reason is explicitly stated in Goal 3 of the six national education goals established at the first education summit in Charlottesville, Virginia. As mentioned previously, Goal 3 explicitly targeted the subjects of English, mathematics, science, history, and geography. In addition, it noted that "every school in America will ensure that all students learn to use their minds well so they may be prepared for responsible citizenship, further learning, and productive employment in our modern economy." (NEGP 1991, p. ix)

There are a number of models a classroom teacher can use to reinforce thinking and reasoning. For example, Quellmalz (1987) has identified four general areas of thinking and reasoning easily adapted to classroom instruction. They are: analyzing,

Figure 5

Portion of Transcript Devoted to Projects at Central Park East Secondary School

Transcript of Portfolios

Please refer to the Curriculum Bulletin for portfolio requirements. A Portfolio is graded on the basis of all items within it as well as knowledge and skill defended before the student's Graduation Committee. Listed below is the title of the student's major work in each area as well as the cumulative grade. Individual portfolio items are available on request.

| Dist | = | Distinguished work | Sat | = | Satisfactorily met requirements |
| MinSat | = | Minimally met requirements | FP | = | Final project (in-depth study) |

The Portfolio

	Grade	Date (completed project)
Post Graduate Plan	Sat	12-90
Autobiography	Sat	12-13-91
Practical Skills and Knowledge (Life Skills)	Dist	3-1-92
Internship (Brookhaven National Lab and Hunter College, NY)	Dist	1-3-91
Ethics, Social Issues, and Philosophy (Controversy of Afrocentric schools)	Dist	2-28-92
Literature (Influences on Malcolm X's life)	Sat+	3-92
History (Events affecting the controversy of Afrocentric schools)	Sat	2-28-92
Geography (Geography of the West Indies)	Sat+	6-5-92
Language other than English (Spanish: English only vs. dual language)	Sat+	1-3-92
Mathematics (Mathematical models: lines and sines)	Dist	3-16-92
Science and Technology (Construction of Expression vectors with Phosphatases 1 and 2A)	Dist	4-92
Fine Arts and Aesthetics (Opera: "Die Fledermaus" and "The Marriage of Figaro")	Sat	12-13-91
Mass Media (Entertainment or News? Our Children's Education)	Sat+	2-24-91
Physical Challenge (Aerobics)	MinSat	6-17-92
Review Date:		

Darling-Hammond, L., and J. Ancess, *Graduation by Portfolio at Central Park East Secondary School* © 1994, p. 20. Reprinted with permission from The National Center for Restructuring Education, Schools, and Teaching (NCREST). Columbia University, New York.

comparing, inferring, and evaluating. Perkins (1992) has identified seven areas of reasoning: explaining, exemplifying, applying, justifying, comparing and contrasting, contextualizing, and generalizing. Marzano and his colleagues (Marzano 1992; Marzano, Pickering, Arredondo, Blackburn, Brandt, and Moffett 1992) have identified a set of fifteen thinking and reasoning skills:

1. Comparing
2. Classifying
3. Induction
4. Deduction
5. Error analysis
6. Constructing support
7. Abstracting
8. Analyzing perspective
9. Decision making
10. Definitional investigation
11. Historical investigation
12. Projective investigation
13. Problem solving
14. Experimental inquiry
15. Invention

Whether a teacher uses these processes or those identified by Quellmalz, those identified by Perkins, those identified by some other theorist, or those identified by the school or district, it is important that students are explicitly taught the steps involved in the processes. This is because students might not understand what exactly is expected of them when they are asked to compare, classify, construct support, and so on. This was rather dramatically illustrated in a study conducted by the National Assessment of Educational Progress (NAEP). A representative sample of 17-year-olds was asked to compare the diet of the frontiersmen with their own diet. They were provided with the diet of the frontier people, and assuming that they were well aware of their own diet, the task primarily called on their abilities to compare. Astonishingly, only 27 percent of the students performing the task received a score of "adequate" or better (Mullis et al. 1990). When the responses of the 73 percent of students who did not receive a score of at least adequate were analyzed, researchers found that the students did not actually compare the items. Rather, most simply made lists of what they ate and what the frontiersmen ate. Apparently, they did not realize that when asked to compare items, they should:

1. identify the characteristics of the items to be compared and explain why these characteristics are important
2. describe how characteristics of the items are similar and different.

The lack of understanding on the part of the students regarding the expectations around simple skills such as the fifteen listed above, led Marzano and his colleagues to identify specific steps associated with the process for comparison:

1. What do I want to compare?
2. What is it about them that I want to compare?

3. How are they the same?
4. How are they different?

As simple as these steps are, they provide students with guidance in understanding what is expected when they are asked to compare, classify, and so on. (Steps for all fifteen processes are presented in Appendix A.)

Regardless of the exact processes used, we believe it important to provide students with explicit guidance in the form of steps such as those above.

Communication Skills. By their very nature, performance tasks and portfolios involve communication, because they usually require some demonstration or "exhibition" of knowledge. Simply stated, exhibitions are "presentations" of student work, or, as assessment expert Grant Wiggins notes, exhibitions call on students to present the fruits of their work (in Willis 1996). Education reporter Scott Willis (1996) describes exhibitions in the following way:

> Typically [exhibitions are] multimedia in nature: students may have to write a paper, make an oral presentation, build a model or create computer graphics, and respond spontaneously to questions. Often, exhibitions are a "culminating" performance. The audience for exhibitions may include teachers, classmates, younger students, parents, or other community members. (p. 1)

Given the importance of communication to performance tasks, teaching and reinforcing general communication skills will quite naturally help students' performance on these tasks. Marzano, Pickering, and McTighe (1993) have identified a number of communication skills commonly included in performance tasks:
- expresses ideas clearly
- communicates effectively with diverse audiences
- communicates effectively in a variety of ways
- communicates effectively for a variety of purposes.

We consider each of these briefly. Clarity of expression is central to all forms of communication. Whether the communication is attempted in a written essay, an oral report, an audiotaped report, or another similar form, ideas must be presented with a clear main point or theme and the appropriate supporting detail. If any communication skill is superordinate to the rest, it may be clarity of expression.

Another aspect of effective communication is the ability to communicate with diverse audiences. In school, those audiences should include peers, parents, experts, novices, the general public, and school board members. As students mature, they increase the types of audiences with which they can effectively communicate. While a primary student might be able to communicate with parents and teachers only, a high school student should be able to communicate with a wide span of audiences. According to current theory in rhetoric (Durst and Newell 1989), communicating effectively with any given audience demands a sensitivity to the level of knowledge of that audience and the interests of its members. Sensitivity to audience also involves adjusting the tone and style of communication so that it is appropriate for the receiver and the context in which it is received. Not considering these important aspects results in a communication that, although logically cohesive, probably will not be easily interpreted or enjoyed by the audience.

Skilled communicators also meet the standard of communicating in a variety of ways. Most schools emphasize two basic forms of communication, writing and speaking. In an information society, however, many other forms of communication are useful and appropriate:

- oral reports
- videotapes
- written reports
- panel discussions
- dramatic enactments
- outlines
- debates
- graphic representations
- newscasts
- discussions
- audiotapes
- flowcharts
- slide shows.

All of these are effective tools for communicating information. Sometimes, however, learners may want to communicate emotion in addition to or in lieu of information, and choose to use other methods of communication:

- collages
- dances
- plays
- songs
- paintings
- photographs
- sculptures.

Being an effective communicator, then, involves a facility with a variety of forms of communication.

Finally, effective communicators must also be able to communicate for a variety of purposes—for instance, to inform, to persuade, to generate questions, or to elicit sympathy, anger, humor, pride, or joy. Researchers have shown that people who have the ability to write for specific purposes have some knowledge of specific rhetorical conventions (Durst and Newell 1989). Effective communicators understand and apply such conventions.

Lifelong Learning Skills. As their name indicates, lifelong learning skills deal with competencies that are used throughout life in a variety of contexts. Such competencies are commonly associated with the world of work. Among others, lifelong learning skills include the following:

- demonstrating the ability to work toward the achievement of group goals
- demonstrating effective interpersonal skills

- restraining impulsivity
- seeking multiple perspectives
- setting and managing progress toward goals
- persevering
- pushing the limits of one's abilities.

For additional lifelong learning skills, see Costa (1984) and Marzano (1992).

Lifelong learning skills gained national prominence when the Secretary's Commission on Achieving Necessary Skills (SCANS) published the report *What Work Requires of Schools: A SCANS Report for America 2000* (1991). The commission spent one year "talking to business owners, to public employees, to the people who manage employees daily, to union officials, and to workers on the line and at their desks. We have talked to them in their stores, shops, government offices, and manufacturing facilities" (p. v). Most of those surveyed agreed that American students must be taught the skills and abilities necessary to be productive members of the work force—skills like those listed above. A complimentary work to the SCANS report, entitled *Workplace Basics: The Essential Skills Employers Want* (Carnevale, Gainer, and Meltzer 1990), was published by the American Society for Training and Development (ASTD). The set of skills identified in this work was almost identical to that articulated in the SCANS report.

The importance of lifelong learning skills is also a common theme among parents. The polling firm, Public Agenda, surveyed a representative sample of parents regarding what should be taught in the schools. Their report is entitled *First Things First: What Americans Expect From Public Schools* (Farkas, Friedman, Boese, and Shaw 1994). It noted that 88 percent of those surveyed said, among other things, that schools should teach and reinforce work-related competencies, such as punctuality, dependability, and self-discipline.

Finally, it appears that educators have reached the same opinion about lifelong learning skills. Specifically, the American Association of School Administrators polled 55 noted educators, referred to as the "Council of 55," regarding what schools should teach to prepare students for the 21st century. The council identified interpersonal skills, including being part of a team, as critical to success in the next century (Uchida, Cetron, and McKenzie 1996).

In summary, lifelong learning skills appear to be valued by all of those constituent groups directly and indirectly related to education.

Helping Students Create Performance Tasks

How can a teacher help reinforce thinking and reasoning skills, communication skills, and lifelong learning skills in the classroom? One of the best ways is to help students design their own performance tasks that incorporate these elements. Marzano, Pickering, and McTighe (1993) have developed a useful process that involves the following steps:

Step 1. Have students identify a question related to something in the cu rent unit of study that interests them.

When students construct their own performance tasks, they usually do so by identifying a question that interests them. We have found providing students with questions cued to the thinking and reasoning processes discussed previously can generally aid this process. These student-oriented questions are listed in Figure 6.

To illustrate how these questions might be used, let us assume that a student is studying about John F. Kennedy. When asked to create a performance task, the student begins by identifying a question from the list in Figure 6 that he wants to answer by studying Kennedy. After examining the list, the student identifies the question "What would have happened if John F. Kennedy had not been assassinated?" In effect, the student has identified a possible event he wants to explore. This question is the foundation of the student's performance task.

Step 2. Help students write a first draft of the task that makes explicit one or more of the reasoning processes listed in Figure 6.

Using the basic question identified by the student, the teacher helps him write a first draft of the performance task. His first draft might read as follows:

> I'm going to examine what might have happened if John F. Kennedy had not been assassinated. I will identify what other people have written about this possibility and then take and defend my own position.

Critical to this step in the process of helping students construct their own performance tasks is identifying, in detail, what they will do as they answer the question they have selected. Recall from the previous discussion that the steps to the reasoning processes listed in Figure 6 are reproduced in Appendix A. To illustrate how these might provide guidance to teachers and students, let us consider the elements of the reasoning process the student has selected to study John F. Kennedy. That process is called "projective investigation." As described in Appendix A, it involves the following steps:

1. Clearly identify the hypothetical event.
2. Identify what is already known or agreed upon about the event.
3. Identify and explain the contradictions and confusions about the event.
4. Develop and defend a plausible resolution to the confusion or contradiction.

Note that in generating his performance task about John F. Kennedy, the student has clearly included elements from 2, 3, and 4 above.

Step 3. Help students identify effective communication skills that will be used in the performance task.

The student now considers the communication skills he might want to incorporate into his performance task. Recall from the previous discussions that the following are the general communication skills commonly included in performance tasks:

- expressing ideas clearly
- communicating effectively with diverse audiences
- communicating effectively in a variety of ways
- communicating effectively for a variety of purposes.

Figure 6

Reasoning Processes That Can Be Used to Generate Performance Activities

Stimulus Question	Reasoning Process
Do you want to determine how certain things are similar and different?	Comparing
Do you want to organize things into groups? Do you want to identify the rules or characteristics that have been used to form groups?	Classifying
Are there specific pieces of information that you want to draw conclusions about?	Induction
Are there specific rules you see operating here? Are there things that you know must happen?	Deduction
Are there errors in reasoning you want to describe? Are there errors being performed in a process?	Error Analysis
Is there a position you want to defend on a particular issue?	Constructing Support
Do you see a relationship that no one else has seen? What is the abstract pattern or theme that is at the heart of the relationship?	Abstracting
Are there differing perspectives on an issue you want to explore?	Analyzing Perspectives
Is there an important decision that should be studied or made?	Decision Making
Is there some new idea or new theory that should described in detail?	Definitional Investigation
Is there something that happened in the past that should be studied?	Historical Investigation
Is there a possible or hypothetical event that should be studied?	Projective Investigation
Do you want to describe how some obstacle can be overcome?	Problem Solving
Is there a prediction you want to make and then test?	Experimental Inquiry
Is there something you want to improve upon? Is there something new you want to create?	Invention

R.J. Marzano, D.J. Pickering, and J. McTighe. *Assessing Student Outcomes*. Alexandria, Va.: Association for Supervision and Curriculum Development. © 1993. Reprinted with permission.

Using this list or another generated by the district, school, or by the individual teacher, the student selects one that fits best with his task. For the purpose of this discussion, let us assume that the student has selected the skill of expressing his or her ideas clearly.

Step 4. Helping students identify a lifelong learning skill they wish to incorporate in their performance task.

Lifelong learning is the final area for students to consider when designing their performance tasks. As we have seen, the list of lifelong learning skills is quite diverse. For illustrative purposes, we will assume that the student working on the John F. Kennedy task has elected to work with others. Consequently, he might decide to incorporate the following lifelong learning skill into the task: "the ability to work toward group goals."

Step 5. Help students rewrite the task so that it highlights all skill areas.

Once the student has identified all elements that will be involved in the task, he rewrites the task to make these areas explicit. The student in our example would rewrite the task in the following way:

> I'm going to examine what might have happened if John F. Kennedy had not been assassinated. I will identify what other people have written on this topic. Working with two other people who have identified similar topics, I will gather information from various sources. While working with my research partners, I will keep track of how well I monitor my behavior in the group. As I collect my research information, I will keep track of the most relevant information and information that is interesting but not as relevant, and report on this information. After I have collected enough information, I will take a position and defend it, taking special care to express my ideas clearly.

Step 6. After students have completed the task, provide them with feedback on each component of the task.

Critical to the effectiveness of a student's learning while engaged in a performance task, is the feedback he or she receives relative to the skills inherent in the task. Four components appear to be involved in the task the same student has created:

1. an understanding of the critical aspects of John F. Kennedy's presidency
2. the ability to perform the mental process involved in projective investigation
3. the ability to express ideas clearly
4. the ability to exhibit leadership in a group.

Students should receive specific and independent feedback in each of these four areas. In the next section we will describe in detail how a teacher might score a performance task like the John F. Kennedy sample; however, we might briefly note that the most effective technique is to describe levels of performance—commonly referred to as a rubric—for each component of the task. The student or students working on this task would receive a rubric score for each of the four areas of the task. Each score should be assigned independently from the other three. Teachers, with the aid of students, can develop their own rubrics for the various parts of a performance. Additionally, they can adopt general rubrics that have been devised by others. As an aid to classroom teachers, we have provided general rubrics for the reasoning processes in Appendix B. Rubrics for the communication skills, and the lifelong learning skills are provided in Appendix C.

Summary

In this section we have discussed two indirect approaches to implementing standards. If a school or district uses an external test as the primary method of implementing standards, then teachers should be made aware of the content covered in the test so that they can address the content in their courses. If a school or district employs performance tasks and portfolios as the primary way of implementing standards, then teachers should systematically provide students with practice in thinking and reasoning skills, communication skills, and lifelong learning skills by helping them design and complete their own performance tasks.

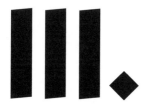

III.

DIRECT APPROACHES TO IMPLEMENTING STANDARDS

Direct approaches to implementing standards necessitate a change in classroom practice for teachers. Additionally, the specific standards that must be addressed in a given class are mandated. Teachers cannot pick and choose those standards they will address.

Step 1. Organize Your Content Around Standards

The first task of a classroom teacher who desires to or must report students' performance on specific standards is to identify the specific standards to be addressed in a unit of instruction along with the specific content within each standard. This task is made fairly easy if the school, district, or state department of education has developed benchmarks at specific grade levels. Benchmarks identify the specific knowledge or skill that should be addressed within a specific standard. Below are the grade 6-8 benchmarks for the Florida Department of State (1996) "sunshine" standard in science entitled "The student understands the basic principles of atomic theory" :
- The student describes and compares the properties of particles and waves.
- The student knows the general properties of the atom (a massive nucleus of neutral neutrons and positive protons surrounded by a cloud of negative electrons) and accepts that single atoms are not visible.
- The student knows that radiation, light, and heat are forms of energy used to cook food, treat diseases, and provide energy.

Benchmarks such as these provide teachers with specific guidance as to what to cover in their courses.

The sunshine standard would provide an eighth grade teacher in the state of Florida with a great deal of guidance regarding the specific content to cover for this standard. We have found that the more guidance provided to individual teachers regarding the content they should cover, the better.

Step 2. Plan the Types of Assessment that Will Be Used for the Various Standards

Ultimately, judgments must be made about student performance on each of the standards addressed in a unit of instruction. To make judgments, information must be gathered on each student regarding his or her performance on each standard. Another term for "gathering information about student performance" is *assessment*. Unfortunately, many educators think of assessment in a very narrow way—when they think of assessing students, they immediately assume that they must design a test. In fact, virtually any method of gathering information about student achievement can be thought of as assessment. Recent years have seen a veritable explosion of types of assessment recommended for classroom use. We have noticed that different types of assessment are useful for different types of content, as shown in Figure 7.

Figure 7 provides a rating (H = high, M = medium, L = low) of the various types of classroom assessment in terms of their utility for different types of knowledge and skill standards. Various forms of classroom assessment are effective for some types of knowledge, but not others. We consider each type.

Figure 7

Rating of the Types of Assessment for Different Types of Standards

Standards	Forced-Choice Items	Essay Questions	Performance Tasks	Teacher Observation	Student Self-Assessment
Subject-specific declarative knowledge	H	H	H	M	H
Subject-specific procedural knowledge	L	H	H	H	H
Thinking and reasoning skills	L	H	H	M	H
Communication skills	L	H	H	L	H
Lifelong learning skills	L	M	M	H	H

H=High
M=Medium
L=Low
© 1997 by McREL Institute. Reprinted with permission.

Forced-Choice Items

Stiggins (1994) defines forced-choice items in the following way:

> This is the classic objectively scored paper and pencil test. The respondent is asked a series of questions, each of which is accompanied by a range of alternative responses. The respondent's task is to select either the correct or the best answer from among the options. The index of achievement is the number or proportion of questions answered correctly. (p. 84)

Although we have limited our discussion of forced-choice tests thus far to those utilizing multiple-choice items, Stiggins lists four types of forced-choice items: (1) multiple-choice items, (2) true/false items, (3) matching exercises, and (4) short answer fill-in-the-blank items.

As explained by Stiggins (1994), short answer fill-in-the-blank items are counted in this category because they only allow for a single answer, which is counted either right or wrong. Teachers commonly use forced-choice items (along with essay items) to design their quizzes, homework assignments, midterm examinations, and final examinations. Such items play a major role in classroom assessment. There are some educators who mistakenly believe that forced-choice formats should be totally discarded in favor of formats that require students to construct personal responses from what they know and understand. These educators fail to acknowledge that forced-choice tests have an important role in the assessment process. To understand this role, it is useful to understand the difference between two primary categories of knowledge: declarative and procedural.

Many cognitive psychologists make the distinction between these primary types of knowledge (Anderson 1982, 1983, 1990a, 1990b, 1993, 1995; Fitts 1964; Fitts and Posner 1967; Frederiksen 1977; Newell and Simon 1972; Norman 1969; Rowe 1985; van Dijk 1980). Declarative knowledge is best thought of as information and usually involves component parts. For example, knowledge of the concept of an "average" involves an understanding of rudimentary information about the concept of distributions, about the concept of a range of scores, and so on. Procedural knowledge consists of skills, strategies, and processes. For example, calculating the average for a group of scores involves the basic computation skills of addition, subtraction, multiplication, and division.

These two types of knowledge are highly interactive. Consequently, students might have gaps in their knowledge if one type is ignored. For example, a student might be able to compute an average for a set of data, but not understand what the average or mean tells about the data set. Conversely, a student might understand the information conveyed by the mean, but not be able to compute a mean efficiently.

As Figure 7 illustrates, forced-choice items are fairly straightforward and effective ways of assessing students' understanding of declarative knowledge particularly when that knowledge is at a factual level. To illustrate, the National Center for Research on Evaluation Standards and Student Testing (CRESST) at UCLA recommends that students complete short-answer items in the following content prior to answering a complex essay question about the Lincoln-Douglas debates:

- popular sovereignty
- Dred Scott
- Missouri Compromise
- bleeding Kansas
- state's rights
- federalism
- underground railroad
- abolitionists. (Baker et al. 1992, pp. 15-16)

Short-answer items that address factual information about topics such as the Dred Scott decision, the Missouri Compromise, and the like, allow the essay question to address the broader aspects of this historical period.

Forced-choice items can be used to assess some types of procedural knowledge. Specifically, procedures that require the execution of specific steps performed in a specific order are amenable to forced-choice items. Such procedures are called algorithms. For example, addition, subtraction, multiplication, and division are algorithms in nature. A teacher could assess those skills using forced-choice items. However, more complex procedures cannot be assessed effectively through forced-choice items. For example, the process of writing does not lend itself to assessment through a forced-choice format.

Essay Questions

Essay questions have long been a staple for classroom teachers (Durm 1993). They can be used effectively to assess both declarative and procedural subject-area knowledge as well as the use of thinking and reasoning skills. When used to assess declarative knowledge, they are commonly designed to test students' understanding of the big ideas—concepts and generalizations—and the relationships among those ideas.

One way to optimize the effectiveness of essay questions is to provide students with information that they react to and use to construct their responses. This practice helps take the emphasis off the strict recall of information. For example, as part of a history examination, CRESST provides students with the original transcripts from the Lincoln-Douglas debates (Baker, Aschbacher, Niemi, and Sato 1992). The following paragraphs are excerpts from these transcripts.

Stephen A. Douglas
Mr. Lincoln tells you, in his speech made at Springfield, before the Convention which gave him his unanimous nomination, that—

"A house divided against itself cannot stand."

"I believe this government cannot endure permanently, half slave and half free."

"I do not expect the Union to be dissolved, I don't expect the house to fall; but I do expect it will cease to be divided."

"It will become all one thing or all the other."

That is the fundamental principle upon which he sets out in this campaign. Well, I do not suppose you will believe one word of it when you come to examine it carefully, and see its consequences. Although the Republic has existed from 1789 to this day, divided into Free States and Slave States, yet we are told that in the future it cannot endure unless they shall become all free or all slave. For that reason he says. . .

Abraham Lincoln

Judge Douglas made two points upon my recent speech at Springfield. He says they are to be the issues of this campaign. The first one of these points he bases upon the language in a speech which I delivered at Springfield which I believe I can quote correctly from memory. I said there that "we are now far into the fifth year since a policy was instituted for the avowed object, and with the confident promise, of putting an end to slavery agitation; under the operation of that policy, that agitation had not only not ceased, but had constantly augmented." "I believe it will not cease until a crisis shall have been reached and passed. 'A house divided against itself cannot stand.' I believe this Government cannot endure permanently, half slave and half free." "I do not expect the Union to be dissolved"—I am quoting from my speech—"I do not expect the house to fall, but I do expect it will cease to be divided. It will become all one thing or the other. Either the opponents of slavery will arrest the spread of it and place it where the public mind shall rest, in the belief that it is in the course of ultimate extinction, or its advocates will push it forward until it shall become alike lawful in all the States, North as well as South.". . .

With this information as a backdrop to which all students have access, the following essay item is presented:

Imagine that it is 1858 and you are an educated citizen living in Illinois. Because you are interested in politics and always keep yourself well-informed, you make a special trip to hear Abraham Lincoln and Stephen Douglas debating during their campaigns for the Senate seat representing Illinois. After the debates you return home, where your cousin asks you about some of the problems that are facing the nation at this time.

Write an essay in which you explain the most important ideas and issues your cousin should understand. Your essay should be based on two major sources: (1) the general concepts and specific facts you know about American History, and especially what you know about the history of the Civil War; (2) what you have learned from the readings yesterday. Be sure to show the relationships among your ideas and facts. (Baker et al. 1992, p. 23)

Note that the task specifically requires students to comment on general concepts and relationships among ideas—elements not easily assessed by forced-choice items. Essay questions, then, are most appropriate for assessing big ideas and relationships among ideas within declarative knowledge, whereas forced-choice items are better suited for lower level factual information. Figure 7 indicates that essay questions can also be used to assess procedural knowledge fairly effectively. This is accomplished by asking students to explain or critique a procedure. To illustrate, consider the CRESST chemistry example below:

> Imagine you are taking a chemistry class with a teacher who has just given the demonstration of chemical analysis you read about earlier.
>
> Since the start of the year, your class has been studying the principles and procedures used in chemical analysis. One of your friends has missed several weeks of class because of illness and is worried about a major exam in chemistry that will be given in two weeks. This friend asks you to explain everything that she will need to know for the exam.
>
> Write an essay in which you explain the most important ideas and principles that your friend should understand. In your essay you should include general concepts and specific facts you know about chemistry, and especially what you know about chemical analysis or identifying unknown substances. You should also explain how the teacher's demonstration illustrates important principles of chemistry.
>
> Be sure to show the relationships among the ideas, facts, and procedures you know. (Baker et al. 1992, p. 29)

Although it is certainly true that a more direct assessment of a student's knowledge of the procedures involved in chemical analysis would require students to actually demonstrate these procedures, this essay question will provide a teacher with valid insights into students' skills in chemical analysis. In fact, research by Shavelson and his colleagues (Shavelson and Baxter 1992; Shavelson, Gao, and Baxter 1993; Shavelson and Webb 1991; Shavelson, Webb, and Rowley 1989) has shown that this indirect assessment of procedural skills correlates highly with more direct, hands-on types of assessments.

Thinking and reasoning skills are also effectively assessed through essay questions. In Section II, we discussed the use of the following thinking and reasoning skills:

1. Comparison
2. Classification
3. Induction
4. Deduction
5. Error Analysis
6. Constructing Support
7. Abstraction
8. Analyzing Perspectives
9. Decision Making
10. Definitional Investigation

11. Historical Investigation
12. Projective Investigation
13. Problem Solving
14. Experimental Inquiry
15. Invention

When these reasoning processes are applied to declarative knowledge in an essay format, a student must demonstrate competence in both the declarative knowledge and the thinking and reasoning process. For example, assume that a teacher wished to construct an essay examination around the information in the Lincoln-Douglas debates that also utilizes a specific thinking and reasoning skill or skills. That essay question might be structured in the following way:

> Douglas and Lincoln said many things in their debates. Identify their areas of agreement as well as their areas of disagreement. Then, select one of their areas of disagreement and analyze the arguments each has presented to determine which one has presented the best case. In your analysis, look at the logic of each argument as well as the accuracy of their information.

This essay actually assesses three elements regarding the Lincoln-Douglas debates, two of which deal with thinking and reasoning and one that deals with declarative knowledge:

1. Students' ability to compare (see thinking and reasoning skill #1)
2. Students' ability to analyze errors (see thinking and reasoning skill #5)
3. Students' understanding of the accuracy of the information presented by Lincoln and Douglas.

Finally, Figure 7 indicates that essay questions can be used effectively to assess communication skills. Clearly, a student's written response to the essay question about Douglas and Lincoln could be used to make judgments about the student's ability to express his or her ideas clearly or to demonstrate other general communication skills.

In summary, essay questions can provide rich assessment information across a number of types of knowledge.

Performance Tasks

We have already discussed performance tasks in some depth in Section II. As our previous discussion and Figure 7 illustrate, they are useful for assessing a variety of types of knowledge. An insightful question to ask is: What is the difference between an essay question and a performance task? In fact, a good essay question is a performance task. More specifically, an essay question is a type of performance task if it combines declarative knowledge with one or more reasoning processes. The previous essay question about the Lincoln-Douglas debates was, in fact, a performance task. If, however, the essay question had simply asked students to retell the important events in the Lincoln-Douglas debates, it would simply have been assessing students' declarative knowledge of those historical events; by our definition this would not have qualified as a performance task because of an absence of knowledge application via the use of one or more thinking and reasoning skills.

The only type of knowledge not well-suited to assessment via performance tasks is lifelong learning skills. We have given performance tasks a rating of medium for lifelong learning skills because a teacher certainly can obtain some valuable information about student competence in this domain using performance tasks. Lifelong learning skills, however, are best assessed through more direct forms of observation.

Teacher Observation

One of the most straightforward ways of collecting assessment data is through informal observation of students. Some educators like reading expert Yetta Goodman, refer to this as "kid watching" (Goodman 1978; Wilde 1996). Quite simply, when observing students, a teacher makes note of their competence as they go about their daily business. This is the most "unobtrusive" way of collecting assessment data because the teacher does not design a special assignment or test to assess students. Stiggins (1994) provides the following example of how a teacher might observe a student relative to social interaction skills that might be part of a school or district's lifelong learning standard:

A primary-grade teacher might watch a student interacting with classmates and draw inferences about that child's level of development in social interaction skills. If the levels of achievement are clearly defined in terms the observer can easily interpret, then the teacher, observing carefully, can derive information from watching that will aid in planning strategies to promote further social development. Thus, this is not an assessment where answers are counted right or wrong. Rather, like the essay test, we rely on teacher judgment to place the student's performance somewhere on a continuum of achievement levels ranging from very low to very high. (p. 160)

As Figure 7 indicates, teacher observation is most appropriate for procedural knowledge and lifelong learning skills, because competence in both these areas can be demonstrated through observable behaviors. For example, a teacher can observe a student demonstrating the ability to read a map—a procedure important to the subject area of geography. Similarly, a teacher can observe a student demonstrating leadership in a group—a lifelong-learning procedural skill.

Student Self-Assessment

Perhaps the most useful form of assessment data is student self-assessment. As the name indicates, this type of data comes directly from the student. Wiggins (1993a) so strongly advocates student self-assessment that one of his nine postulates for a more thoughtful assessment system is "Postulate 4: An authentic education makes self-assessment central." (p. 53)

Hansen (1994) notes that self-assessment is central to the development of higher order metacognitive skills. Additionally, she postulates that self-assessment leads to the identification of individual learning goals, which are at the heart of the assessment process:

> Self-evaluation leads to the establishment of goals. That is what evaluation is for. We evaluate in order to find out what we have learned so we will know what to study next. People who self-evaluate constantly ask themselves, "Where am I going? Am I getting there? Am I getting somewhere? Am I enjoying the trip? Is this worthwhile? Do I approve of the way I'm spending my time?" (p. 37)

Another useful tool in terms of student self-assessment is the student learning log. When using a learning log, the student records his or her perceptions of his or her progress in the standards and benchmarks covered in the class. A sample student log is presented in Figure 8.

The student is asked to provide information—a self-evaluation and the evidence that supports it for a specific topic—in this case, declarative knowledge about the Lincoln-Douglas debates. The student then writes both evaluation and evidence in his or her log. Finally, this log is used by the student in an assessment conference held with the teacher during the grading period.

Some parents, and even some educators, question the validity of student self-assessment assuming that students will always provide inflated assessments of their own understanding and skill. Experiences of those who have made extensive use of student self-assessment do not support these fears. For example, Linda Darling-Hammond, Jacqueline Ancess, and Beverly Falk (1995) report that in their studies students have

Figure 8
Sample Student Log

My evaluation of my understanding of the Lincoln-Douglas debates	My evaluation is based on the following evidence
I think I have a fairly good grasp of the Lincoln-Douglas debates. I would rate myself as very competent in this topic.	My oral report on the debate included information that neither Lincoln nor Douglas specifically said. I had to take what they actually did say and combine it with information I knew about that particular situation to come up with some new ideas about the debate.

© 1996 by McREL Institute. Reprinted with permission.

demonstrated a "clear-headed capacity" to evaluate their own work (p. 155). Middle school teachers Lyn Countryman and Merrie Schroeder (1996) report that students' candor in making self-assessments was noted by parents. After hearing her child's self-assessment, one mother remarked, "I feel our child was more honest with us than most teachers would be" (p. 68). Another parent commented, "Students seem more open and honest about their performance. I didn't get the sugar-coated reports from advisors who tend to present negative aspects in a positive manner" (p. 68).

Assessment Conferences

Ultimately, the teacher must put together the various types of assessment data collected in a classroom. To facilitate this process, we recommend a conference between teacher and student. The purpose of this conference is for the teacher to share the assessment data he or she has collected on the student and for the student to share his or her self-assessment data. Assessment specialist Doris Sperling (1996) and curriculum theorist David Hawkins (1973) both refer to this type of interaction as collaborative assessment. Wiggins (1993a) notes that a collaborative approach is inherent in the very derivation of the word assess:

> The etymology of the word *assess* alerts us to this clinical—that is, client-centered—act. *Assess* is a form of the Latin verb *assidere*, to "sit with." In an assessment, one "sits with" the learner. It is something we do *with* and *for* the student, not something we do to the student. The person who "sits with you" is someone who "assigns value"—the "assessor" (hence the earliest and still current meaning of the word, which relates to tax assessors). But interestingly enough, there is an intriguing alternative meaning to that word, as we discover in *The Oxford English Dictionary*: this person who "sits beside" is one who "shares another's rank or dignity" and who is "skilled to advise on technical points." (p. 14)

We believe that Wiggins' comments capture the true spirit of effective assessment: teacher and student jointly analyzing the student's strengths and weaknesses relative to specific learning outcomes.

The specifics of conducting a student/teacher assessment conference are neither complex nor new. In fact, within the whole language movement such conferences have been standard fare for at least two decades (see Atwell 1987; Calkins 1986; Cazden 1986; Hansen 1987; Staton 1980; Thaiss 1986; Valencia 1987; Young and Fulwiler 1986). Briefly, within an assessment conference, the teacher presents his or her evaluation of a student's performance on specific standards along with his or her evidence used to form his or her judgments (e.g., quizzes, projects, and observations). Similarly, the student presents his or her evaluation of his or her performance on specific standards and the evidence he or she has used to form that judgment. If the teacher is using a specific scale for performance levels on specific skills—like those presented in Appendix B—then the student evaluates himself or herself using exactly the same scale. Any discrepancies between the teacher's rating and the student's rating on specific standards or benchmarks are then discussed in depth with the intent of coming to the most accurate judgment regarding the student's understanding and skill.

Step 3. Organize Your Grade Book Around Standards

One convention that is critical to the type of assessment and record-keeping described in this section is that a teacher's grade book is organized around standards. The most straightforward way of thinking about a grade book organized around standards is that the columns of the grade book are dedicated to standards rather than to assignments, tests, and activities (see Figure 9).

Note that the grade book has room for six standards. With a foldout page there is room for 12 standards. Space is provided at the top of the grade book for the teacher to keep track of different assessments, activities, and homework assignments used for grading. Our sample grade book lists seven items:

A. Homework: September 7
B. Quiz: September 9
C. Performance Task: September 14
D. Quiz: September 16
E. Homework: September 21
F. Performance Task: September 23
G. Unit Test: September 25

Notice that in this marking period the teacher has given two graded homework assignments, two quizzes, two performance tasks, and one unit test. These assessments have been used to assess six standards that deal with the following content:

Standard #1: percolation
Standard #2: soil
Standard #3: bar graphs
Standard #4: hypothesis testing
Standard #5: working with groups
Standard #6: oral presentations

Also note that assessment item K is the student's self-assessment for his or her performance on each standard. As described previously, the teacher entered this into the grade book at the time of the teacher/student assessment conference during which each student provided the teacher with his or her personal judgments on each standard and the evidence for the student's judgment.

Each box below each standard contains room for the teacher to enter a number reflecting his or her judgments about the student's performance on each standard for a specific assessment, activity, homework assignment, and so on. For example, consider James Barton's scores for standard 2, information about soil. This box has a number of rows, each preceded by a letter. The letter in each row represents the assignment, the test, or the event that the teacher used to make judgments about

Figure 9

Sample Unit Grade Book

Standards:		#1 Understands percolation	#2 Understands soil information	#3 Designs and uses bar graphs	#4 Generates and tests a hypothesis	#5 Contributes to groups	#6 Makes an oral presentation
Carmen Adams	A	4	4				
	B	3	4	4			
	C	4			4	4	
	D	4	4	3			4
	E	4	3	4			
	F	3		4			4
	G	4	4	4			
	H						
	I						
	J						
	K	4	4	4	3	3	4
	L	4 3	4	4	4 4 4 4	4 4	4 4
		4	**4**	**4**	**4**	**4**	**4**
James Barton	A	2	2				
	B	2	3	2			
	C	3			3	3	
	D	2	2	2			2
	E	2	3	2			
	F	1		3			1
	G	2	3	2			
	H						
	I						
	J						
	K	3	3	3	3	3	3
	L	1 2	2 3	2 3	1 1	2 2	2 2
		2	**3**	**2**	**2**	**2**	**2**
Michael Caruso	A	3	3				
	B	3	3	3			
	C	4			3	3	
	D	2	2	4			4
	E	3	3	4			
	F	3		4			4
	G	3	3	3			
	H						
	I						
	J						
	K	3	4	3	3	4	3
	L	3 3	3 3	4 4	3 3	4 3	4
		3	**3**	**4**	**3**	**4**	**4**

James's performance on standards. The number represents the teacher's judgment about James's performance on each of the assessments for each applicable standard. Note that most of the assessments cover more than one standard. For example, consider assessment A—the quiz given on September 7. The quiz provided assessment information for standard 1 and standard 2.

It is important to note that some standards have far more entries than others. In fact, every assessment that was given covered information about standard 1. This indicates that the teacher was quite consciously emphasizing this standard. Finally, note that row L is used to record the teacher's informal observations on each standard. For example, the teacher made two informal observations about James's performance on standard 1. The teacher assigned a score of 1 on one occasion and a score of 2 on the other.

The use of columns in a grade book to represent standards, instead of assignments, tests, and activities, is a major shift in thinking for teachers. Under this system, when an assessment is designed, the teacher must think in terms of the standards it is intended to address. If a quiz is given that covers three standards, then the teacher makes three entries in the grade book for each student—one entry for each standard—as opposed to one overall entry for the entire quiz. Teachers who have tried this approach assert that it makes them plan their assessments much more carefully. Instead of simply assigning questions at the end of a chapter for homework or constructing a set of forced-choice items to form a quiz, the teacher must continually ask him or herself, About which standards am I trying to obtain assessment information? and, What's a good way to obtain that information?

An equally radical change in grading is the use of numbers that represent levels of performance as opposed to points to total the number of correct responses. Note that in Figure 9 all entries for a given assessment are either 1, 2, 3, or 4. This is because the teacher has used performance levels like those in Figures 10 and 11.

Note that Figure 10 is a general rubric for procedural knowledge. If the standard that is being addressed is primarily declarative (i.e., informational), then the teacher should use the rubric in Figure 11. For example, assume that standard 2 in Figure 9 about soil is primarily informational in nature. Notice that the quiz on September 9 (see row B) addressed this standard (along with standards 1 and 3). Based on that quiz, the teacher's judgment was that James Barton demonstrated an understanding of the important information in the quiz about soil and can exemplify that information in some detail. That corresponds to a level 3 on the generic scale for declarative knowledge. If the student had demonstrated incomplete knowledge relative to soil, but did not have severe misconceptions, the teacher would have assigned a score of 2. The generic rubric in Figure 11, then, must be translated in terms of the specific declarative knowledge assessed on a quiz, homework assignment, and/or other task or activity. This is also the case for the generic rubric pertaining to procedural knowledge. To illustrate, consider standard 3 that deals with designing and interpreting bar graphs—knowledge that is highly procedural in nature. Again, the quiz on September 9th was designed to assess this procedural standard. Based on James Barton's performance on that quiz, the teacher judged that the student made a number of errors when carrying out the procedures involved in designing or using

	Figure 10
	**Scale for Performance on a Procedural Benchmark**
Scale	**Performance Criteria**
4	Advanced Performance: Carries out the major processes/skills inherent in the procedure with relative ease and automaticity
3	Proficient Performance: Carries out the major processes/skills inherent in the procedure without significant error, but not necessarily at an automatic level
2	Basic Performance: Makes a number of errors when carrying out the processes and skills important to the procedure, but still accomplishes the basic purpose of the procedure
1	Novice Performance: Makes so many errors when carrying out the process and skills important to the procedure that it fails to accomplish its purpose

	Figure 11
	**Scale for Performance on a Declarative Benchmark**
Scale	**Performance Criteria**
4	Advanced Performance: Demonstrates a thorough understanding of the important information, is able to exemplify that information in detail and articulate complex relationships and distinctions
3	Proficient Performance: Demonstrates an understanding of the important information; is able to exemplify that information in some detail
2	Basic Performance: Demonstrates an incomplete understanding of the important information, but does not have severe misconceptions
1	Novice Performance: Demonstrates an incomplete understanding along with severe misconceptions

bar graphs, but still accomplished the basic procedure. This corresponds to a level 2 in the generic rubric. If James Barton had carried out the major steps involved in the process of designing and utilizing bar graphs, the teacher would have assigned a score of 3 and so on. If thinking and reasoning skills and/or communication skills and/or lifelong-learning skills are taught and assessed within a grading period, then the teacher would use the rubrics in Appendices B and C. For example, the teacher might have used the rubric in Appendix C for working with groups to make judgments about his or her students on the fifth standard.

The key feature in this approach is that the teacher makes multiple judgments over a grading period regarding each student's understanding and/or skill relative to the knowledge in specific standards. To do this, the teacher must translate performance on a specific test, assignment, task, or activity into a judgment of the student's level of understanding or skill. If a quiz is administered, the teacher considers the set of items that deal with each standard and makes judgments relative to each student's level of performance; the teacher does not simply add up the number of correct items that pertain to each standard.

Some noneducators, and even some educators, react suspiciously to the role that teacher judgment plays in this system. They assume that it introduces an element of subjectivity into grading. What these critics commonly fail to realize is that the current system is inherently subjective. Citing the research of others (e.g., Ornstein 1994), Guskey (1996b) notes that "regardless of the method used, assigning grades or reporting on student learning is inherently subjective" (p. 17). In a similar vein, educator Carl Glickman (1993) explains that current grading practice provides a false sense of objectivity by the sometimes complex manipulation of numbers to arrive at grades.

The extensive use of tests and the scores associated with those tests does not necessarily produce sound assessments of student understanding and skill. We assert that well-informed judgment is a much more robust and powerful tool. As Wiggins (1993a) explains:

> Judgment certainly does not involve the unthinking application of rules or algorithms—the stock in trade of all conventional tests. Dewey uses the words "knack, tact, cleverness, insight, and discernment" to remind us that judgment concerns "horse sense"; someone with good judgment is someone with the capacity to "estimate, appraise and evaluate." (Dewey adds, not coincidentally, "with tact and discernment.") The effective performer, like the good judge, never loses sight of either relative importance or the difference between the "spirit" and the "letter" of the law or rules that apply. Neither ability is testable by one-dimensional items, because to use judgment one must ask questions of foreground and background as well as perceive the limits of what one "knows." (pp. 219-220)

Guskey (1996b) adds further evidence for the validity and utility of teacher judgment. Citing the research of others (e.g., Brookhart 1993; O'Donnell and Woolfolk 1991), Guskey concludes:

> Because teachers know their students, understand various dimensions of students' work, and have clear notions of the progress made, their subjective perceptions may yield very accurate descriptions of what students have learned. (pp. 17-18)

The final judgment a teacher must make during a grading period is to assign an overall score representing a student's understanding and skill for each standard addressed during the grading period. This is entered into the white box in the lower portion of each column of the grade book. For example, in Figure 9, James Barton received an overall score of 3 for the standard about soil (see column 2). Teachers should carefully think through how many will arrive at this overall score. We believe that teachers should weight some entries higher than others when computing the overall score on a standard. Specifically, we assert that the teacher should consider heavily the student's self-assessment (entry K for each standard in the grade book). In addition, many researchers and theorists (e.g., Conley 1996; Fitzpatrick, Kulieke, Hillary, and Begitschke 1996; Guskey 1996b; Herman 1996; Marzano, Pickering, and McTighe 1993; McTighe and Ferrera 1996; Mitchell 1992; Mitchell and Neill 1992; Spady 1988, 1995; Wiggins 1993a, 1993b, 1994) recommend placing heavy emphasis on the most recent information. Guskey (1996b) explains:

> The key question is, "what information provides the most accurate depiction of students' learning at this time?" In nearly all cases, the answer is "The most current information." If students demonstrate that past assessment information no longer accurately reflects their learning, that information must be dropped and replaced by new information. (p. 21)

The overall score for a standard should be a representation of what the student knows and can do at the end of a unit of instruction. Teachers should think of scores accumulated during the unit as pieces of information, some more valid than others.

Step 4. Assign Grades Based on Student's Performance on Standards

Ultimately, a teacher will probably have to provide an overall grade for students. At some point in the future, report cards with summary scores for each standard, but without overall letter grades, might be accepted within the American culture; however, at the present time, it is probably advisable (for political reasons only) to provide overall grades for courses even though individual scores on standards provide adequate information about student competence in specific standards.

Once a teacher has assigned a final performance level for each standard being assessed, he or she can combine these in some way to construct an overall grade. At this stage, weight can be applied to the various standards. To illustrate, assume that our model teacher has assigned the weights depicted in Figure 12.

Here the teacher has given a weight of 2 to standards 1, 3, and 5, thus giving these standards more quantitative influence in the final grade. These weights would be assigned to standards prior to the beginning of the grading period and communicated to students at the very beginning of the grading period. Upon assigning summary scores for each student on each standard, the teacher would then apply the weights to each standard. This is depicted in Figure 13 for the student Ashley Walker.

Figure 12
Weights Applied to Various Standards

Standard		Weight
1.	Percolation	2
2.	Soil	1
3.	Bar Graphs	2
4.	Hypothesis Testing	1
5.	Working with Groups	2
6.	Oral Presentations	1

Figure 13
Computation of Total Quality Points for a Sample Student

Student Name: Ashley Walker

Standard	Student Score	Weight	Quality Points
1	3	2	6
2	3	1	3
3	3	2	6
4	1	1	1
5	3	2	6
6	2	1	2
	Totals	9	24

Note that the quality points for Ashley have been calculated by multiplying her score on a standard by the weight assigned to the standard. An average score can be calculated for each student at the end of the grading period by using the following formula:

$$\frac{\text{Total Quality Points}}{\text{Total of Weights}}$$

In Ashley's case, her total quality points are 24. The total weights applied to the six standards are 9. (This is the sum of column 3 in Figure 13.) To determine Ashley's average score on the weighted standards, the teacher would divide Ashley's total quality points (24) by the total weight (9), for an average of 2.67. This is the average score, based on a scale of 1 through 4, that Ashley received in the six standards addressed where some standards were weighted more heavily than others.

The next step is to convert each student's average score into an overall grade. The teacher might decide on the following conversion system:

3.26-4.00	=	A
2.76-3.25	=	B
2.01-2.75	=	C
1.50-2.00	=	D
1.49 or below	=	F

In this system, Ashley's average score of 2.67 would be assigned the grade of C.

The reader might have the reaction that the cutoff points for the various grades appear arbitrary. In fact, they are. This is one of the greatest weaknesses of using overall letter grades, as Guskey (1996b) explains:

> The cutoff between grade categories is always arbitrary and difficult to justify. If the scores for a grade of B range from 80-89 for example, a student with a score of 89 receives the same grade as the student with a score of 80 even though there is a 9-point difference in their scores. But the student with a score of 79—a 1-point difference—receives a grade of C because the cutoff for a B grade is 80. (p. 17)

Guskey's comments also apply to the conversion system above. For example, a student who had received one more quality point than Ashley (25 quality points instead of Ashley's 24) would have an overall score of 2.78 which would have translated into a grade of B. In other words, if Ashley had received one score higher in any one of the six standards, she would have been assigned a B rather than a C.

From this discussion, it should be obvious that using overall grades to report students' progress on standards is not our preferred method. As measurement expert Richard Stiggins (1994) notes, a single symbol—a single letter grade—simply cannot adequately summarize all of the complex learning involved in a course of study. Unfortunately, overall letter grades are used in almost every district from the middle school on up and they are probably here to stay for quite some time. Consequently, if a school or district has no option but to use overall letter grades to report students' performance on standards at the classroom level, then we recommend the following guidelines:

1. Use well-informed teacher judgment to assign scores that represent levels of understanding and skill for specific standards as opposed to assigning scores to homework, quizzes, midterms, final tests, and other tasks and activities and then simply combining these scores.

2. Have a written grading policy for each course that clearly describes how scores on standards are to be weighted.
3. Clearly communicate to students and parents which standards are included in the computation of grades and how those standards are weighted.

These guidelines will help make overall letter grades more representative of students' performance on specific standards. This approach, however, is a compromise solution at best. The preferred method is to report performance on individual standards in lieu of a single letter grade.

If a school or district has the option to report performance on individual standards, it will need to change its report cards to reflect the scores on each standard.

Changing Report Cards to Reflect Scores on Specific Standards

Direct approaches require that classroom teachers attend to specific standards on which they must report student achievement. This drastically changes the nature and format of report cards. For example, consider the sample report card in Figure 14 in which each teacher has provided an overall grade for a student in his or her course as well as scores on individual standards. Also note that teachers have used a four-point scale with the levels: novice, basic, proficient, and advanced. This could have been a three-point scale, a five-point scale, or another rating scale. The scale selected to report student achievement on standards is less important than the fact that all teachers are using the same scale.

The report card in Figure 14 can be thought of as dual-purpose in that it provides students and parents with the overall letter grade with which they are so familiar, at the same time that it provides them with ratings on specific standards. Note that with this approach, there will probably be some repetition of standards from course to course. This generally occurs with the reasoning, communication, and lifelong learning standards discussed in Section II. Such standards commonly cut across all content areas. For example, in Figure 14, both of the courses in mathematics and science have addressed logic and reasoning.

A report of students' performance on individual standards calls for a transcript that does the same. Figure 15 contains a sample transcript based on standards. Note that in the first column scores on standards represent an average. This assumes that students have been assessed on individual standards more then once. The number of times each standard has been assessed is shown in the column to the right of the average score. For example, mathematics standard 5 on probability has been assessed three times; the average score is 1.7. The transcript also shows the lowest score received on this standard (1), the highest score (3), and the most recent score (3). Of particular interest to some are the most recent scores, which represent the classroom assessment of the student's most recent performance on standards. (For a discussion, see Guskey 1996a.) One policy decision a school or district should make is whether to compute overall performance on a set of standards using the most recent scores or all of the scores. The transcript in Figure 15 does both.

Figure 14

Sample Report Card: Reporting Student Performance by Grade and by Standard

Nobel County School District 1: George Washington High School Student Progress Report

Name: Al Einstein
Address: 111 E. McSquare Dr.
City: Relativity, Colorado 80000
Grade Level: 11

Course Title	Grade
Algebra II and Trigonometry	C-
Advanced Placement Physics	A+
U.S. History	B-
American Literature	C+
Physical Education	B-
Chorus	B+
Geography	B-
Current GPA:	2.81
Cumulative GPA:	3.23

Standards Ratings

Algebra II and Trigonometry

		Novice (1)	Basic (2)	Proficient (3)	Advanced (4)
Mathematics Standard 1:	Numeric Problem Solving	(1)			
Mathematics Standard 2:	Computation	(1)			
Mathematics Standard 3:	Measurement		(2)		
Mathematics Standard 4:	Geometry		(2)		
Mathematics Standard 5:	Probability		(2)		
Mathematics Standard 6:	Algebra	(1)			
Mathematics Standard 7:	Data Analysis		(2)		
Reasoning Standard 5:	Decision Making		(2)		
Lifelong Learning Standard 4:	Self-regulation	(1)			

Overall Mathematics: 1.6

Figure 14 (continued)

Standards Ratings

Advanced Placement Physics

		Novice (1)	Basic (2)	Proficient (3)	Advanced (4)
Science Standard 1:	Earth Features				(4)
Science Standard 2:	Earth Processes			(3)	
Science Standard 3:	The Universe				(4)
Science Standard 4:	Diversity of Life				(4)
Reasoning Standard 4:	Princ. of Scientific Inquiry				(4)
Lifelong Learning Standard 1:	Working with Groups			(3)	
Overall Science:	3.7				

U.S. History

		Novice (1)	Basic (2)	Proficient (3)	Advanced (4)
History Standard 1:	Civilization and Society		(2)		
History Standard 2:	Exploration and Colonization			(3)	
History Standard 3:	Revolution and Conflict				(4)
History Standard 4:	Industry and Commerce		(2)		
History Standard 5:	Forms of Government		(2)		
Reasoning Standard 3:	Identifying Similarities and Differences			(3)	
Lifelong Learning Standard 3:	Leadership Skills			(3)	
Overall History:	2.7				

American Literature

		Novice (1)	Basic (2)	Proficient (3)	Advanced (4)
Language Arts Standard 1:	The Writing Process		(2)		
Language Arts Standard 2:	Usage, Style, and Rhetoric			(3)	
Language Arts Standard 3:	Research: Process and Product			(3)	
Language Arts Standard 4:	The Reading Process		(2)		
Language Arts Standard 5:	Reading Comprehension			(3)	
Language Arts Standard 6:	Literary/Text Analysis		(2)		
Language Arts Standard 7:	Listening and Speaking		(2)		
Language Arts Standard 8:	The Nature of Language		(2)		

American Literature

		Novice (1)	Basic (2)	Proficient (3)	Advanced (4)
Language Arts Standard 9:	Literature	(1)			
Reasoning Standard 1:	Principles of Argument				(4)
Lifelong Learning Standard 5:	Reliability and Responsibility		(2)		
Overall Language Arts:	2.4				

Figure 14 (continued)

Standards Ratings

Physical Education

	Novice (1)	Basic (2)	Proficient (3)	Advanced (4)
Physical Education Standard 1: Movement Forms: Theory and Practice		(2)		
Physical Education Standard 2: Motor Skill Development			(3)	
Physical Education Standard 3: Physical Fitness: Appreciation			(3)	
Physical Education Standard 4: Physical Fitness: Application		(2)		
Reasoning Standard 6: Decision Making			(3)	
Lifelong Learning Standard 1: Working with Groups		(2)		
Overall Physical Education: 2.5				

Chorus

	Novice (1)	Basic (2)	Proficient (3)	Advanced (4)
Music Standard 1: Vocal Music			(3)	
Music Standard 2: Instrumental Music			(3)	
Music Standard 3: Music Composition			(3)	
Music Standard 4: Music Theory		(2)		
Music Standard 5: Music Appreciation				(4)
Reasoning Standard 3: Identifying Similarities and Differences			(3)	
Lifelong Learning Standard 2: Working with Individuals			(3)	
Overall Music: 3.0				

Geography

	Novice (1)	Basic (2)	Proficient (3)	Advanced (4)
Geography Standard 1: Places and Regions		(2)		
Geography Standard 2: Human Systems			(3)	
Geography Standard 3: Physical Systems			(3)	
Geography Standard 4: Uses of Geography		(2)		
Geography Standard 5: Environment and Society			(3)	
Geography Standard 6: The World in Spatial Terms		(2)		
Reasoning Standard 2: Logic and Reasoning			(3)	
Lifelong Learning Standard 5: Working with Groups		(2)		
Overall Geography: 2.5				

R.J. Marzano and J.S. Kendall, *A Comprehensive Guide to Designing Standards-Based Districts, Schools, and Classrooms.* Alexandria, Va.: Association for Supervision and Curriculum Development, © 1996. Reprinted with permission.

The Inherent Danger in Changing Report Cards

When a school or district elects to adopt a new report card and transcript like those in Figures 14 and 15, it generally does so at some risk. Education reporter Lynn Olson (1995b) documents what can happen when a school district attempts to change the traditional grading and reporting practices. She describes the case of a district in Rhode Island in which parents, administrators, and volunteer community members worked for two years to develop a report card that evaluated students on relatively specific information and skills. To the surprise of those on the report card committee, some parents reacted quite negatively to the new approach even though it had undergone extensive study and testing. Olson (1995b) dramatizes the opposition:

> The three women seated around Dona LeBouef's butcherblock kitchen table look more like a bevy of P.T.A. moms than a rebel army. Dressed in coordinated shirts and pants and denim jumpers, they're articulate and polite. Classical music plays softly in the background as they sip their coffee and review the weapons in their campaign: a large sheaf of photocopied newspaper articles and editorials, old report cards, and petitions.
>
> Their target is pilot report cards introduced by the public school system here last fall that eliminated traditional letter grades in the elementary schools. The new format, tested citywide, was designed to more accurately reflect the teaching going on in the classroom and to provide families with more detailed information about their children. School officials thought parents would be pleased. They were wrong. (p. 23)

Olson explains that parents were upset because they were used to the ABC format. Simply stated, the new report cards did not look enough like what parents were used to. Even in the face of evidence that the new grading system format was much more accurate and informative, a relatively small group of parents was able to marshal support from some 1,300 community members in the form of a petition. As Olson (1995b) notes:

> At issue is one of the most sacred traditions in American education: the use of letter grades to denote student achievement. The truth is that letter grades have acquired an almost cultlike importance in American schools. They are the primary shorthand tool for communicating to parents how children are faring. (p. 24)

In spite of the opposition that a district or school might encounter by reporting by individual standards, we believe it is worth the struggle and the effort it might take. As Wiggins (1994) notes, "Using a single grade with no clear and stable meaning to summarize all aspects of performance is the problem. We need more, not fewer, grades and more efficient kinds of grades if the parent is to be informed." (p. 29)

One of the advantages of the report card in Figure 14 is that it provides parents and students with an overall grade—which they are used to—and specific scores on

Figure 15
Sample Transcript: Reporting Student Performance by Standard

Subject and Standards Rated Average	Average Rating	Number of Ratings	Most Recent Rating	Highest Rating	Lowest Rating
Subject: MATHEMATICS					
Standard 1: Numeric Problem Solving	1.7	3	3	3	1
Standard 2: Computation	1.3	3	2	2	1
Standard 3: Measurement	2.7	3	2	3	2
Standard 4: Geometry	1.5	2	2	2	1
Standard 5: Probability	1.7	3	3	3	1
Standard 6: Algebra	1.0	2	1	1	1
Standard 7: Data Analysis	3.0	1	3	3	3
Overall Mathematics	1.84	17	2.28	3	1
Subject: SCIENCE					
Standard 1: Earth and Space	4.0	4	4	4	4
Standard 2: Life Sciences	3.5	2	4	4	3
Standard 3: Physical Sciences	3.5	4	4	4	2
Standard 4: Science and Technology	3.75	4	4	4	3
Overall Science	3.69	14	4.0	4	2
Subject: HISTORY					
Standard 1: Civilization and Human Society	2.75	4	3	3	2
Standard 2: Exploration and Colonization	3.0	3	3	3	3
Standard 3: Revolution and Conflict	3.75	3	3	4	3
Standard 4: Industry and Commerce	2.3	3	3	3	1
Standard 5: Forms of Government	3.0	2	2	4	2
Overall History	2.96	15	2.8	4	1
Subject: GEOGRAPHY					
Standard 1: Places and Regions	2.0	2	1	3	1
Standard 2: Human Systems	3.75	4	3	4	3
Standard 3: Physical Systems	2.5	4	3	3	2
Standard 4: Uses of Geography	3.5	2	4	4	3
Standard 5: Environment and Society	3.0	3	4	4	2
Standard 6: The World in Spatial Terms	2.5	2	3	3	2
Overall Geography	2.88	17	3.0	4	1
Subject: LANGUAGE ARTS					
Standard 1: The Writing Process	2.6	7	3	3	2
Standard 2: Usage, Style, and Rhetoric	3.0	9	4	4	2
Standard 3: Research: Process and Product	2.8	5	4	4	2
Standard 4: The Reading Process	2.6	5	2	3	2
Standard 5: Reading Comprehension	3.6	9	2	4	2
Standard 6: Literary/Text Analysis	2.8	6	3	3	2
Standard 7: Listening and Speaking	3.5	10	4	4	3

Figure 15 (continued)

Sample Transcript: Reporting Student Performance by Standard

Subject and Standards Rated Average	Average Rating	Number of Ratings	Most Recent Rating	Highest Rating	Lowest Rating
Subject: LANGUAGE ARTS (continued)					
Standard 8: The Nature of Language	3.0	3	4	4	2
Standard 9: Literature	2.0	3	2	2	2
Overall Language Arts	2.88	57	3.1	4	2
Subject: THE ARTS/MUSIC					
Standard 1: Vocal Music	2.0	2	3	3	1
Standard 2: Instrumental Music	3.3	3	3	4	3
Standard 3: Music Composition	2.0	2	2	2	2
Standard 4: Music Theory	3.0	2	2	4	2
Standard 5: Music Appreciation	4.0	3	4	4	4
Overall Music	2.86	12	2.8	4	1
Subject: PHYSICAL EDUCATION					
Standard 1: Movement Forms: Theory and Practice	2.3	3	2	3	2
Standard 2: Motor Skill Development	2.0	4	3	3	1
Standard 3: Physical Fitness: Appreciation	3.75	4	4	4	3
Standard 4: Physical Fitness: Application	2.0	4	3	3	1
Overall Physical Education	2.5	15	3.0	4	1
Subject: REASONING					
Standard 1: The Principles of Argument	3.7	10	4	4	2
Standard 2: Logic and Reasoning	3.0	10	4	4	2
Standard 3: Identifying Similarities and Differences	3.0	12	4	4	2
Standard 4: Principles of Scientific Inquiry	3.6	3	4	4	3
Standard 5: Techniques of Problem Solving	3.8	13	4	4	3
Standard 6: Techniques of Decision Making	3.2	13	4	4	2
Overall Reasoning	3.4	61	4.0	4	2
Subject: LIFELONG LEARNING SKILLS					
Standard 1: Working with Groups	2.8	17	3	3	2
Standard 2: Working with Individuals	3.01	17	4	4	2
Standard 3: Leadership Skills	2.7	14	3	3	2
Standard 4: Self-regulation	2.6	13	3	3	1
Standard 5: Reliability and Responsibility	3.0	17	3	3	3
Overall Lifelong Learning Skills	2.82	78	3.2	4	1
All subject areas combined	2.87	286	3.1	4	1

R.J. Marzano and J.S. Kendall. *A Comprehensive Guide to Designing Standards-Based Districts, Schools, and Classrooms.* Alexandria, Va.: Association for Supervision and Curriculum Development. © 1996. Reprinted with permission.

specific standards—which they are not used to. Obviously, this type of record-keeping requires changes in classroom practice.

Conclusion

In this book, we have attempted to describe the various approaches to standards-based education and the advantages and disadvantages of those approaches. Perhaps more importantly, we have attempted to explain how each approach can and should affect what happens in individual classrooms. In our opinion, one of the biggest mistakes a teacher can make is to ignore the standards movement. To do this is to put individual students at great risk in that they might not be adequately prepared to meet the challenges that standards-based education will certainly impose on them.

APPENDIX A

Steps to Reasoning Processes

These processes are adapted from *Assessing Student Outcomes* by R. J. Marzano, D. Pickering, and J. McTighe. Copyright © 1993 by McREL Institute. Reprinted with permission.

Reasoning Process 1: Comparison

Comparison involves describing the similarities and differences between two or more items. The process includes three components that can be assessed:

a. Selecting appropriate items to compare.
b. Selecting appropriate characteristics on which to base the comparison.
c. Accurately identifying the similarities and differences among the items, using the identified characteristics.

Reasoning Process 2: Classification

Classification involves organizing items into categories based on specific characteristics. The process includes four components that can be assessed:

a. Selecting significant items to classify.
b. Specifying useful categories for the items.
c. Specifying accurate and comprehensive rules for category membership.
d. Accurately sorting the identifying items into the categories.

Reasoning Process 3: Induction

Induction involves creating a generalization from implicit or explicit information and then describing the reasoning behind the generalization. The process includes three components that can be assessed:

a. Identifying elements (specific pieces of information or observations) from which to make inductions.
b. Interpreting the information from which inductions are made.
c. Making and articulating accurate conclusions (inductions) from the selected information or observations.

Reasoning Process 4: Deduction

Deduction involves identifying implicit or explicit generalizations or principles (premises) and then describing their logical consequences. The process includes three components that can be assessed:

a. Identifying and articulating a deduction based on important and useful generalizations or principles implicit or explicit in the information.
b. Accurately interpreting the generalizations or principles.
c. Identifying and articulating logical consequences implied by the identified generalizations or principles.

Reasoning Process 5: Error Analysis

Error analysis involves identifying and describing specific types of errors in information or processes. It includes three components that can be assessed:

a. Identifying and articulating significant errors in information or in a process.
b. Accurately describing the effects of the errors on the information or process.
c. Accurately describing how to correct the errors.

Reasoning Process 6: Constructing Support

Constructing support involves developing a well-articulated argument for or against a specific claim. The process includes three components that can be assessed:

a. Accurately identifying a claim that requires support rather than a fact that does not require support.
b. Providing sufficient or appropriate evidence for the claim.
c. Adequately qualifying or restricting the claim.

Reasoning Process 7: Abstracting

Abstracting involves identifying and explaining how the abstract pattern in one situation or information set is similar to or different from the abstract pattern in another situation or information set. The process includes three components that can be assessed:

a. Identifying a significant situation or meaningful information that is useful as a subject for the abstracting process.
b. Identifying a representative general or abstract pattern for the situation or information.
c. Accurately articulating the relationship between the general or abstract pattern and another situation or information set.

Reasoning Process 8: Analyzing Perspectives

Analyzing perspectives involves considering one perspective on an issue and the reasoning behind it as well as an opposing perspective and the reasoning behind it.

The process includes three components that can be assessed:

a. Identifying an issue on which there is disagreement.
b. Identifying one position on the issue and the reasoning behind it.
c. Identifying an opposing position and the reasoning behind it.

Reasoning Process 9: Decision Making

Decision making involves selecting among apparently equal alternatives. It includes four components that can be assessed:

a. Identifying important and appropriate alternatives to be considered.
b. Identifying important and appropriate criteria for assessing the alternatives.
c. Accurately identifying the extent to which each alternative possesses the appropriate criteria.
d. Making a selection that adequately meets the decision criteria and answers the initial decision question.

Reasoning Processes 10, 11, and 12: Investigation

Investigation is a process involving close examination and systematic inquiry. There are three basic types of investigation:

- *Definitional Investigation:* Constructing a definition or detailed description of a concept for which such a definition or description is not readily available or accepted.
- *Historical Investigation*: Constructing an explanation for some past event for which an explanation is not readily available or accepted.
- *Projective Investigation:* Constructing a scenario for some future event or hypothetical past event for which a scenario is not readily available or accepted.

Each type of investigation includes three components that can be assessed:

a. Accurately identifying what is already known or agreed upon about the concept (definitional investigation), the past event (historical investigation), or the future event (projective investigation).
b. Identifying and explaining the confusions, uncertainties, or contradictions about the concept (definitional investigation), the past event (historical investigation), or the future event (projective investigation).
c. Developing and defending a logical and plausible resolution to the confusions, uncertainties, or contradictions about the concept (definitional investigation), the past event (historical investigation), or the future event (projective investigation).

Reasoning Process 13: Problem Solving

Problem solving involves developing and testing a method or product for overcoming obstacles or constraints to reach a desired outcome. It includes four components that can be assessed:

a. Accurately identifying constraints or obstacles.
b. Identifying viable and important alternatives for overcoming the constraints or obstacles.
c. Selecting and adequately trying out alternatives.
d. If other alternatives were tried, accurately articulating and supporting the reasoning behind the order of their selection, and the extent to which each overcame the obstacles or constraints.

Reasoning Process 14: Experimental Inquiry

Experimental inquiry involves testing hypotheses that have been generated to explain a phenomenon. It includes four components that can be assessed:

a. Accurately explaining the phenomenon initially observed using appropriate and accepted facts, concepts, or principles.
b. Making a logical prediction based on the facts, concepts, or principles underlying the explanation.
c. Setting up and carrying out an activity or experiment that effectively tests the prediction.
d. Effectively evaluating the outcome of the activity or experiment in terms of the original explanation.

Reasoning Process 15: Invention

Invention involves developing something unique or making unique improvements to a product or process to satisfy an unmet need. It includes four components that can be assessed:

a. Identifying a process or product to develop or improve to satisfy an unmet need.
b. Identifying rigorous and important standards or criteria the invention will meet.
c. Making detailed and important revisions in the initial process or product.
d. Continually revising and polishing the process or product until it reaches a level of completeness consistent with the criteria or standards identified earlier.

APPENDIX B

Rubrics for Reasoning Processes

These rubrics are adapted from *Assessing Student Outcomes* by R. J. Marzano, D. Pickering, and J. McTighe. Copyright © 1993 by McREL Institute. Reprinted with permission.

Reasoning Process 1: Comparison

Comparison involves describing the similarities and differences between two or more items. The process includes three components that can be assessed:

a. Selecting appropriate items to compare.

4 Selects items that are entirely suitable for addressing the basic objective of the comparison and that show original or creative thinking.

3 Selects items that provide a means for successfully addressing the basic objective of the comparison.

2 Selects items that satisfy the basic requirements of the comparison, but create some difficulties for completing the task.

1 Selects items that are inappropriate to the basic objective of the comparison.

b. Selecting appropriate characteristics on which to base the comparison.

4 Selects characteristics that encompass the most essential aspects of the items and present a unique challenge or provide an unusual insight.

3 Selects characteristics that provide a vehicle for meaningful comparison of the items and address the basic objective of the comparison.

2 Selects characteristics that provide for a partial comparison of the items and may include some extraneous characteristics.

1 Selects characteristics that are trivial or do not address the basic objective of the comparison. Selects characteristics on which the items cannot be compared.

c. Accurately identifying the similarities and differences among the items, using the identified characteristics.

4 Accurately assesses all identified similarities and differences for each item on the selected characteristic. Additionally, the student provides inferences from the comparison that were not explicitly requested in the task description.

3 Accurately assesses the major similarities and differences among the identified characteristics.

2 Makes some important errors in identifying the major similarities and differences among the identified characteristics.

1 Makes many significant errors in identifying the major similarities and differences among the identified characteristics.

Reasoning Process 2: Classification

Classification involves organizing items into categories based on specific characteristics. The process includes four components that can be assessed:

a. Selecting significant items to classify.

4 Specifies the items to be classified and selects significant items that present some interesting challenge in classification.

3 Selects significant items for classification that present some challenge in classification.

2 Selects items of little significance or presents a routine sorting problem.

1 Selects trivial items or items that have no relationship to the task.

b. Specifying useful categories for the items.

4 Creates categories that provide a useful way of looking at the items at an unusual level of depth.

3 Creates categories that focus on the significant characteristics of the items.

2 Creates categories that provide for some analysis of the items but may not include all the important characteristics of the items.

1 Creates categories that address only trivial aspects of the items.

c. Specifying accurate and comprehensive rules for category membership.

4 Provides a clear and complete specification of the defining characteristics of each category. Describes the defining characteristics in such a way as to provide a unique or unusual way of looking at the items.

3 Clearly specifies the defining characteristics of the categories and addresses any questions of overlap in characteristics.

2 Describes the defining characteristics of categories in a way that results in some overlap or confusion between categories, or describes characteristics that are unrelated to the rules for category membership.

1 Identifies characteristics that do not accurately describe the categories.

d. Accurately sorting the identified items into the categories.

4 Correctly sorts each of the items into the categories and describes the extent to which each item has the characteristics ascribed to the categories. Describes insights gained during the sorting process.

3 Correctly sorts each of the items into the categories and, when appropriate, describes the extent to which each item has the characteristics ascribed to the categories.

2 Makes some errors in assigning items to their appropriate categories, or does not describe the extent to which each item has the characteristics of the category, when it is clearly appropriate for the task.

1 Makes frequent and significant errors in assigning items to categories and does not show how the items have the characteristics of their assigned categories.

Reasoning Process 3: Induction

Induction involves creating a generalization from implicit or explicit information and then describing the reasoning behind the generalization. The process includes three components that can be assessed:

a. **Identifying elements (specific pieces of information or observations) from which to make inductions.**

4 Clearly and accurately identifies all relevant information from which to make inductions. The type of information selected reflects creative insight and a careful analysis of the situation.

3 Specifies all relevant information from which to make inductions. Selects information that is important to the general topic.

2 Includes some information that is not important to the induction or does not accurately identify the important information from which the induction(s) could be made.

1 Selects unimportant or trivial information for the induction.

b. **Interpreting the information from which inductions are made.**

4 Provides accurate interpretations that illustrate insight into the information from which they were made. The interpretations reflect a study of or a familiarity with the particulars of the topic.

3 Provides interpretations that, with few exceptions, are valid and say something important about the topic.

2 Provides some interpretations that are based on significant misunderstandings of the subject matter.

1 Significantly misinterprets the information. Makes interpretations that have no bearing on the area or are clearly illogical.

c. **Making and articulating accurate conclusions (inductions) from the selected information or observations.**

4 Draws conclusions that reflect clear and logical links between the information or observations and the interpretations made from them. The rationale for the interpretations shows a thoughtful and accurate attention to the process of induction.

3 Presents conclusions that, with few exceptions, follow logically from the selected information or observations.

2 Presents some conclusions that reflect erroneous interpretations made from the information or observations.

1 Draws many erroneous conclusions from the selected information or observations and cannot satisfactorily describe the rationale behind the conclusions.

Reasoning Process 4: Deduction

Deduction involves identifying implicit or explicit generalizations or principles (premises) and then describing their logical consequences. The process includes three components that can be assessed:

a. **Identifying and articulating a deduction based on important and useful generalizations or principles implicit or explicit in the information.**
4 Selects generalizations or principles that show extreme insight into the topic.
3 Selects important generalizations or principles that contribute to the understanding of the material being studied.
2 Selects generalizations or principles that generally relate to the information available but that may not have significant explanatory power.
1 Selects generalizations or principles that do not have significant bearing on the material and do not contribute to the understanding of the subject.

b. **Accurately interpreting the generalizations or principles.**
4 Demonstrates an understanding of the generalizations or principles that is not only accurate but provides a unique perspective on the topic.
3 Demonstrates an understanding of the generalizations or principles that is accurate and contributes to an understanding of the topic.
2 Demonstrates a somewhat inaccurate understanding of the generalizations or principles.
1 Demonstrates an incorrect understanding or interpretation of the generalizations or principles.

c. **Identifying and articulating logical consequences implied by the identified generalizations or principles.**
4 Accurately identifies logical conclusions implied by the generalizations or principles. Recognizes more subtle inferences that could have important effects on the subject area.
3 With few errors, accurately identifies the consequences of the generalizations or principles. The consequences relate closely to the subject area and are worthwhile subjects for discussion.
2 Accounts for important consequences of the generalizations or principles, but identifies consequences that may not be germane to the topic; or makes logical errors in identifying the consequences.
1 Identifies consequences that have little significance and are not logical or germane to the topic.

Reasoning Process 5: Error Analysis

Error analysis involves identifying and describing specific types of errors in information or processes. It includes three components that can be assessed:

a. Identifying and articulating significant errors in information or in a process.

4 Accurately identifies all errors in the information or process under study and makes clear why the points identified are errors. Also identifies subtle but important errors that are difficult to recognize.

3 Accurately identifies all critical errors in the information or process under study and makes clear why the points identified are errors.

2 Fails to recognize some important errors or identifies some points that are not errors.

1 Recognizes only insignificant errors or mistakes valid points for errors.

b. Accurately describing the effects of the errors on the information or process.

4 Provides an accurate analysis of the effects of the errors, including a complete description of the ramifications of the errors beyond the most obvious levels of impact.

3 Provides an accurate analysis of the effects of the errors, omitting few details.

2 Describes the effects of the errors, but omits some important consequences; or does not accurately describe all the effects of the errors.

1 Does not correctly assess the effects of the errors, or describes effects that do not exist.

c. Accurately describing how to correct the errors.

4 Provides a highly thoughtful or creative approach for correcting the errors.

3 Provides a workable way of correcting the errors. The response addresses the major concerns raised by the errors.

2 Provides an approach for correcting the errors. The approach addresses some of the major errors, though it may not be the best or most appropriate response to the situation.

1 Does not accurately describe how to correct the errors.

Reasoning Process 6: Constructing Support

Constructing support involves developing a well-articulated argument for or against a specific claim. The process includes three components that can be assessed:

a. Accurately identifying a claim that requires support rather than a fact that does not require support.

4 Accurately identifies a claim that requires support. The identified claim has been mistaken by many others for a fact that requires no support.

3 Accurately identifies a claim that requires support and does not confuse the claim with any other information.

2 Identifies a claim that requires support but may mistakenly include information that does not require support.

1 Identifies information that does not require support and fails to identify a claim that should have support.

b. Providing sufficient or appropriate evidence for the claim.

4 Presents a clear and accurate treatment of all available evidence that addresses the central point of the claim. Considers what evidence is missing and how it should affect an evaluation of the claim.

3 With no major errors, presents all relevant evidence needed to support the claim.

2 Provides evidence for the claim, but may not address all necessary aspects.

1 Fails to provide convincing evidence for the claim.

c. Accurately qualifying or restricting the claim.

4 Provides careful and reasoned qualifications or restrictions for the claim in such a way that the argument offers a unique perspective on the claim.

3 Provides accurate qualifications or restrictions for the claim, with the result being a well-defended claim.

2 Qualifies or restricts the claim, but leaves out important aspects of the qualifications or restrictions.

1 Does not address qualifications or restrictions for the claim.

Reasoning Process 7: Abstracting

Abstracting involves identifying and explaining how the abstract pattern in one situation or information set is similar to or different from the abstract pattern in another situation or information set. The process includes three components that can be assessed:

a. Identifying a significant situation or meaningful information that is useful as a subject for the abstracting process.

4 Identifies a situation or information that provides a rich source of material for the process of abstracting. The selected information is not commonly used in abstracting tasks but has a pattern that could be quite powerful when abstracted.

3 Identifies significant information that also has a pattern that lends itself to the abstracting process.

2 Identifies information that seems unimportant but does have a pattern that can be used in the abstracting process.

1 Identifies trivial information having no identifiable pattern that can be used in the abstracting process.

b. Identifying a representative general or abstract pattern for the information.

4 Identifies a general or abstract pattern that provides unusual or provocative insights into the information under study. The pattern furnishes the means for seeing other material from a unique perspective.

3 Constructs a general or abstract pattern that accurately represents the information from which it came.

2 Creates a general or abstract pattern that may not be a completely accurate representation of the information or situation from which it was drawn but does

focus on its most important elements.

1 Does not create a general or abstract pattern that accurately represents the information or situation selected.

c. Accurately articulating the relationship between the general or abstract pattern and another situation or information set.

4 Demonstrates creativity in the selection of another situation or information set that contains a similar general or abstract form. The situation or information is important and provides a very good subject for analysis.

3 Correctly identifies another situation or information set that contains the essential characteristics of the general or abstract form and provides a worthwhile subject for study.

2 Identifies another situation or information set that does not perfectly match the general or abstract form but has some similarities.

1 Selects another situation or information set that does not conform in any way to the general or abstract pattern identified.

Reasoning Process 8: Analyzing Perspectives

Analyzing perspectives involves considering one perspective on an issue and the reasoning behind it as well as an opposing perspective and the reasoning behind it. The process includes three components that can be assessed:

a. Identifying an issue on which there is disagreement.

4 Identifies and articulates implicit points of disagreement that are not obvious but are the underlying cause of conflict.

3 Identifies and articulates explicit points of disagreement that cause conflict.

2 Identifies and articulates issues that are not the most important points of disagreement.

1 Ignores explicit and implicit points of disagreement.

b. Identifying one position on the issue and the reasoning behind it.

4 Articulates a detailed position and the reasoning behind it and, if a strong line of reasoning does not underlie the position, articulates the errors or holes in the reasoning.

3 Articulates a position and the basic reasoning underlying the position. Does not address or incompletely addresses the errors or holes in the reasoning.

2 Articulates a position but does not present a clear line of reasoning behind it.

1 Does not articulate a clear position.

c. Identifying an opposing position and the reasoning behind it.

4 Articulates a detailed opposing position and the reasoning behind it. If a strong line of reasoning does not underlie the position, articulates the errors or holes in the reasoning.

3 Articulates an opposing position and the basic reasoning underlying it. Does

not address or incompletely addresses the errors or holes in the reasoning.
2 Articulates an opposing position but does not present a clear line of reasoning behind it.
1 Does not articulate a clear opposing position.

Reasoning Process 9: Decision Making

Decision making involves selecting among apparently equal alternatives. It includes four components that can be assessed:

a. Identifying important and appropriate alternatives to be considered.
4 Presents a comprehensive list of the most important possible alternatives and describes each in detail.
3 Identifies alternatives that represent most of the important possible alternatives.
2 Identifies some alternatives that are important and others that are not.
1 Selects alternatives that are clearly not relevant to the decision.

b. Identifying important and appropriate criteria for assessing the alternatives.
4 Clearly identifies the criteria by which the identified alternatives will be assessed. The criteria reflect an unusually thorough understanding of the nature of the decision task.
3 Clearly identifies the criteria by which the identified alternatives will be assessed. With no significant exceptions, the criteria are important to the decision task.
2 Identifies some important criteria by which the identified alternatives will be assessed. However, some important criteria are omitted, or criteria are included that may not be important to the decision task.
1 Identifies few or no criteria that are relevant to the decision task.

c. Accurately identifying the extent to which each alternative possesses each criteria.
4 Provides a thorough, fully developed assessment of each alternative based upon the criteria. Exceeds the demands of the decision task by comparing and contrasting the alternatives to provide greater insights.
3 Presents an accurate assessment of the extent to which the alternatives possess the identified criteria.
2 Does not completely address all the criteria; or applies all appropriate criteria to the alternatives but is not completely accurate in assessing how well the criteria have been met.
1 Does not address the extent to which the alternatives meet the criteria or is inaccurate is assessing how well the alternatives meet the criteria.

d Making a selection that adequately meets the decision criteria and answers the initial decision question.
4 Selects an alternative that meets or exceeds the criteria and that represents a

well-supported answer to the initial decision question. Provides a useful discussion of issues and insights that arose during the selection process.

3 Successfully answers the decision question by selecting an alternative that meets or exceeds established criteria.

2 Selects an alternative that does not entirely conform to the student's assessment of the alternatives.

1 Makes a selection that does not appear reasonable or cannot be justified by the student's evaluation of the alternatives.

Reasoning Processes 10, 11, and 12: Investigation

Investigation is a process involving close examination and systematic inquiry. There are three basic types of investigation:

- *Definitional Investigation:* Constructing a definition or detailed description of a concept for which such a definition or description is not readily available or accepted.
- *Historical Investigation:* Constructing an explanation for some past event for which an explanation is not readily available or accepted.
- *Projective Investigation:* Constructing a scenario for some future event or hypothetical past event for which a scenario is not readily available or accepted.

Each type of investigation includes three components that can be assessed:

a. **Accurately identifying what is already known or agreed upon about the concept (definitional investigation), the past event (historical investigation), or the future event (projective investigation).**

4 Presents a thorough and correct account of what is already known. Supplying information that may not be commonly known, but that has some bearing on the topic being studied.

3 Presents an accurate account, with no important omissions, of what is already known or agreed upon about the topic being studied.

2 Presents information on what is already known or agreed upon about the topic being studied; however, the information may not be complete in all particulars, or the student may introduce some inaccuracies.

1 Presents little or no accurate and important information about what is already known or agreed upon about the topic.

b. **Identifying and explaining the confusions, uncertainties, or contradictions about the concept (definitional investigation), the past event (historical investigation), or the future event (projective investigation).**

4 Identifies the important confusions, uncertainties, or contradictions surrounding the topic. Brings to light misconceptions or confusions that are commonly overlooked.

3 Identifies, with no important errors, significant confusions, uncertainties or

contradictions surrounding the topic.

2 Identifies confusions, uncertainties, or contradictions associated with the topic. The problems identified include some, but not all, of the most critical issues.

1 Fails to accurately identify any important confusions, uncertainties, or contradictions surrounding the topic.

c. **Developing and defending a logical and plausible resolution to the confusions, uncertainties, or contradictions about the concept (definitional investigation), the past event (historical investigation), or the future event (projective investigation).**

4 Provides a logical and well-developed resolution to the confusions, uncertainties, or contradictions. The resolution reflects creative thinking as well as thoughtful attention to the details of the problem.

3 Presents a clear resolution to the problems associated with the concept. The resolution is a logical and plausible outcome of the investigation.

2 Develops and presents a resolution to the problems associated with the concept. The resolution is satisfactory, but lacks thorough treatment and accuracy.

1 Presents an unsubstantiated and implausible resolution to the confusions, uncertainties, or contradictions.

Reasoning Process 13: Problem Solving

Problem solving involves developing and testing a method or product for overcoming obstacles or constraints to reach a desired outcome. It includes four components that can be assessed:

a. **Accurately identifying constraints or obstacles.**

4 Accurately and thoroughly describes the relevant constraints or obstacles. Addresses obstacles or constraints that are not immediately apparent.

3 Accurately identifies the most important constraints or obstacles.

2 Identifies some constraints or obstacles that are accurate along with some that are not accurate.

1 Omits the most significant constraints or obstacles.

b. **Identifying viable and important alternatives for overcoming the constraints or obstacles.**

4 Identifies creative but plausible solutions to the problem under consideration. The solutions address the central difficulties posed by the constraint or obstacle.

3 Proposes alternative solutions that appear plausible and that address the most important constraints or obstacles.

2 Presents alternative solutions for dealing with the obstacles or constraints, but the solutions do not all address the important difficulties.

1 Presents solutions that fail to address critical parts of the problem.

c. Selecting and adequately trying out alternatives.

4 Engages in effective, valid, and exhaustive trials of the selected alternatives. Trials go beyond those required to solve the problem and show a commitment to an in-depth understanding of the problem.

3 Puts the selected alternatives to trials adequate to determine their utility.

2 Tries out the alternatives, but the trials are incomplete and important elements are omitted or ignored.

1 Does not satisfactorily test the selected solutions.

d. If other alternatives were tried, accurately articulating and supporting the reasoning behind the order of their selection and the extent to which each overcame the obstacles or constraints.

4 Provides a clear, comprehensive summary of the reasoning that led to the selection of secondary solutions. The description includes a review of the decisions that produced the order of selection and how each alternative fared as a solution.

3 Describes the process that led to the ordering of secondary solutions. The description offers a clear, defensible rationale for the ordering of the alternatives and the final selection.

2 Describes the process that led to the ordering of secondary solutions. The description does not provide a clear rationale for the ordering of the alternatives, or the student does not address all the alternatives that were tried.

1 Describes an illogical method for determining the relative value of the alternatives. The student does not present a reasonable review of the strengths and weaknesses of the alternative solutions that were tried and abandoned.

Reasoning Process 14: Experimental Inquiry

Experimental inquiry involves testing hypotheses that have been generated to explain a phenomenon. It includes four components that can be assessed:

a. Accurately explaining the phenomenon initially observed using appropriate and accepted facts, concepts, or principles.

4 Provides an accurate explanation of the phenomenon. The facts, concepts, or principles used for the explanation are appropriate to the phenomenon and accurately applied. The explanation reflects thorough and careful research or understanding.

3 Provides an accurate explanation of the phenomenon. The facts, concepts, or principles used in the explanation are appropriate to the phenomenon and accurately applied, with no significant errors.

2 Explains the phenomenon but misapplies or omits some facts, concepts, or principles that are important for understanding the phenomenon.

1 Leaves out key facts, concepts, or principles in explaining the phenomenon, or does not use appropriate facts, concepts, or principles to explain the phenomenon.

b. Making a logical prediction based on the facts, concepts, or principles underlying the explanation.

4 Makes a verifiable prediction that reflects insight into the character of the phenomenon. The prediction is entirely appropriate to the facts, concepts, or principles used to explain the phenomenon.

3 Makes a prediction that follows from the facts, concepts, or principles used to explain the phenomenon. The prediction can be verified.

2 Makes a prediction that reflects a misunderstanding of some aspects of the facts, concepts, or principles used to explain the phenomenon, or makes a prediction that presents difficulties for verification.

1 Makes a prediction that cannot be verified.

c. Setting up and carrying out an activity or experiment that effectively tests the prediction.

4 Sets up and carries out an activity or experiment that is a complete and valid test of the prediction and addresses all important questions raised by the prediction. The activity or experiment is designed to provide complete and accurate data and a model of the experimental design.

3 Sets up and carries out an activity or experiment that is a fair test of the prediction and addresses the most important questions raised by the prediction. The activity or experiment provides accurate data for evaluation.

2 Sets up and carries out an activity or experiment that addresses some important aspects of the prediction, but omits others. The design of the activity or experiment produces some errors in data collection or interpretation.

1 Sets up and carries out an activity or experiment that does not test the central features of the prediction. The experimental design is seriously flawed and the collection of accurate data is unlikely.

d. Effectively evaluating the outcome of the activity or experiment in terms of the original explanation.

4 Provides a complete and accurate explanation of the outcome of the activity or experiment and does so in terms of the relevant facts, concepts, or principles. Provides insights into the nature of the phenomenon studied or the facts, concepts, and principles used to explain it.

3 Provides a complete explanation of the outcome of the activity or experiment with no important errors. Presents the explanation in terms of the relevant facts, concepts, or principles.

2 Provides a general explanation of the outcome of the activity or experiment but omits one or two important aspects, or may not effectively relate the outcome to the facts, concepts, or principles used to generate the prediction.

1 Provides an inaccurate, highly flawed explanation of how the outcome relates to the original explanation.

Reasoning Process 15: Invention

Invention involves developing something unique or making unique improvements to a product or process to satisfy an unmet need. It includes four components that can be assessed:

a. **Identifying a process or product to develop or improve to meet an unmet need.**
4 Proposes a process or product that provides a unique solution to an unmet need. The proposed process or product reflects a high level of creativity.
3 Proposes a process or product that provides a good answer to the unmet need.
2 Proposes a process or product that will not adequately satisfy the unmet need.
1 Proposes a process or product that has little or no relation to the unmet need.

b. **Identifying rigorous and important standards or criteria the invention will meet.**
4 Sets out rigorous criteria well suited to the purpose of the invention. The student identifies only the highest achievable standards of quality as acceptable outcomes.
3 Establishes an appropriate set of criteria for the invention.
2 Identifies criteria for the invention that may not be completely appropriate for the product or sets standards that do not ensure a worthwhile or completed product.
1 Establishes criteria that fail to address the most important purposes of the invention. Sets standards so low that little quality can be expected.

c. **Making detailed and important revisions to the initial process or product.**
4 Reviews the process or product at a considerable level of detail. The revisions or improvements clearly bring the process or product closer to fulfilling the purpose for which it is designed. The student's attention to the details of the draft or model makes a high-quality product likely.
3 Revises the process or product in ways that serve the purpose of the process or product.
2 Revises the process or product but attempts to address only the most obvious difficulties.
1 Makes few, if any, attempts at revision and appears satisfied with the initial process or product, although obvious difficulties still remain.

d. **Continually revising and polishing the process or product until it reaches a level of completeness consistent with the criteria or standards articulated earlier.**
4 Develops a final process or product that meets the criteria established at a demanding level of quality. The process or product fulfills the purpose for which it was designed. In addition, the process or product reflects creativity and establishes a model for creative work of high quality.
3 Continues revising the process or product until it meets all standards and criteria. The process or product successfully serves the purpose for which it was designed.
2 Revises the process or product until it meets minimum standards.
1 Finishes revising the process or product before it has met minimum standards. The process or product does not meet many important criteria and fails in its purpose.

APPENDIX C

Rubrics for Effective Communication Standards

These rubrics are adapted from *Assessing Student Outcomes* by R. J. Marzano, D. Pickering, and J. McTighe. Copyright © 1993 by McREL Institute. Reprinted with permission.

a. Expresses ideas clearly.
4 Clearly and effectively communicates the main idea or theme and provides support that contains rich, vivid, and powerful detail.
3 Clearly communicates the main idea or theme and provides suitable support and detail.
2 Communicates important information but not a clear theme or overall structure.
1 Communicates information as isolated pieces in a random fashion.

b. Effectively communicates with diverse audiences.
4 Presents information in a style and tone that effectively capitalize on the audience's level of interest and level of knowledge or understanding.
3 Presents information in a style and tone consistent with the audience's level of interest and level of knowledge or understanding.
2 Presents information in a style and tone inappropriate for the audience's level of interest or the audience's level of knowledge.
1 Presents information in a style and tone inappropriate for both the audience's level of interest and level of knowledge.

c. Effectively communicates in a variety of ways.
4 Uses multiple methods of communication, applying the conventions and rules of those methods in highly creative and imaginative ways.
3 Uses two different methods of communication, applying the conventions and rules of those methods in customary ways.
2 Attempts to use two methods of communication but does not apply the conventions and rules of those methods.
1 Uses only one method of communication when more than one method is clearly needed or requested and does not correctly apply the conventions and rules of that method.

d. Effectively communicates for a variety of purposes.
- 4 Clearly communicates a purpose in a highly creative and insightful manner.
- 3 Uses effective techniques to communicate a clear purpose.
- 2 Demonstrates an attempt to communicate for a specific purpose but makes significant errors or omissions.
- 1 Demonstrates no central purpose in the communication or makes no attempt to articulate a purpose.

APPENDIX D

Rubrics for Lifelong Learning Standards

These rubrics are adapted from *Assessing Student Outcomes* by R. J. Marzano, D. Pickering, and J. McTighe. Copyright © 1993 by McREL Institute. Reprinted with permission.

a. Demonstrating the ability to work toward the achievement of group goals.
4 Actively helps identify group goals and works hard to meet them.
3 Communicates commitment to the group goals and effectively carries out assigned roles.
2 Communicates a commitment to the group goals but does not carry out assigned roles.
1 Does not work toward group goals or actively works against them.

b. Demonstrating effective interpersonal skills.
4 Actively promotes effective group interaction and the expression of ideas and opinions in a way that is sensitive to the feelings and knowledge base of others.
3 Participates in group interaction without prompting. Expresses ideas and opinions in a way that is sensitive to the feelings and knowledge base of others.
2 Participates in group interaction with prompting or expresses ideas and opinions without considering the feelings and knowledge base of others.
1 Does not participate in group interaction, even with prompting, or expresses ideas and opinions in a way that is insensitive to the feelings or knowledge base of others.

c. Restraining impulsivity.
4 Carefully considers a situation to determine if more study is required before acting. When further study is required, investigates thoroughly before acting.
3 Considers whether more study is required before acting. When further study is required, gathers sufficient information before acting.
2 Cursorily considers whether more study is required before acting. When further study is required, gathers sufficient information before acting.
1 Does not consider whether more study is required before acting.

d. Seeking multiple perspectives.
4 Seeks out different and opposing points of view. Considers alternative views

impartially and rationally.

3 Is aware of points of view that differ from own. Makes a concerted effort to consider alternative views.

2 Is aware that his or her perspective is not completely shared by all. Pays mild attention to alternative viewpoints.

1 Assumes his or her own perspective is universally accepted. Deliberately avoids other perspectives.

e. Setting and managing progress toward goals.

4 Sets a precise goal. Considers and carries out all necessary subgoals. Creates and adheres to a detailed time line.

3 Sets a goal. Considers and carries out some subgoals. Creates and carries out a useful time line.

2 Begins tasks without a completely defined goal. Makes little attempt to define subgoals or develop a time line.

1 Makes no effort to identify a goal or its related subgoals and time line.

f. Persevering.

4 Demonstrates strong determination in the pursuit of a solution. Monitors his or her level of involvement and develops and uses a number of strategies to keep self on task.

3 Shows determination in the pursuit of a solution. Uses strategies to keep self on track.

2 Makes some effort to resolve a difficult problem but does not spend sufficient time and effort on the problem. Is easily derailed and does not use strategies to keep self on task.

1 Shows evidence of quitting the challenge early, before really trying to solve a problem.

g. Pushing the limits of one's abilities.

4 Seeks out a highly challenging task and works on the task until it is completed or until attaining significant understandings from the task.

3 Accepts the challenge presented and works on the task until it is completed or until attaining significant understandings from the task.

2 Accepts the challenge presented and makes an initial attempt to complete the task, but quits before completing it or attaining significant understandings.

1 Does not accept the challenge.

GLOSSARY

algorithm—a procedure, usually mathematical, in which steps must be performed in a specific order that generally involves repetition; such procedures can be assessed using forced-choice test items.

assessment—the process of gathering information about a student's performance in order to measure or judge that performance.

authentic task—any task that is drawn from a real life situation; contrast with *performance task*.

declarative knowledge—information usually consisting of component parts; contrasted with *procedural knowledge*.

exhibitions—demonstrations of knowledge, typically multimedia in nature.

forced-choice items—questions on a classic objectively scored paper and pencil test accompanied by several alternative responses, one of which is correct or best.

generalizability theory—a theory of measurement that seeks to determine how generalizable a student's performance on one test is to his or her performance on another test of the same subject matter.

metacognitive skills—those skills identified with the most highly developed levels of knowledge.

performance task—any task in which students are asked to apply their knowledge and defend their reasoning regardless of whether that task is one they might undertake in real life; contrasted with *authentic task*.

portfolio assessment—a performance assessment method in which an individual collects and stores in a real or virtual portfolio representative samples of his or her work for submission to a jury or panel of judges for assessment.

procedural knowledge—skills, strategies, and processes required for mastery of a given subject matter; contrasted with *declarative knowledge*.

projective investigation—a reasoning process that involves identifying various elements of a historical problem, and developing and defending a solution to that problem.

teacher observation—a method of collecting assessment data informally; because this method is not related to a designed assignment, it is probably the most "unobtrusive" way of collecting information about a student's performance.

REFERENCES

Airasian, Peter W. 1994. *Classroom assessment.* 2d ed. New York: McGraw-Hill.

Anderson, J.R. 1982. Acquisition of cognitive skills. *Psychological Review* 89: 369-406.

———. 1983. *The architecture of cognition.* Cambridge, Mass.: Harvard University Press.

———. 1990a. *Cognitive psychology and its implications.* New York: W. H. Freeman and Company.

———. 1990b. *The adaptive character of thought.* Hillsdale, N.J.: Lawrence Erlbaum Associates.

———. 1993. *Rules of the mind.* Hillsdale, N.J.: Lawrence Erlbaum Associates.

———. 1995. *Learning and memory: An integrated approach.* New York: John Wiley & Sons.

Archbald, D.A., and F.M. Newmann. 1988. *Beyond standardized testing: Assessing authentic achievement in the secondary school.* Reston, Va.: National Association of Secondary School Principals.

Atwell, N.C. 1987. *In the middle.* Portsmouth, N.H.: Heinemann.

Baker, E.L., P.R. Aschbacher, D. Niemi, and E. Sato. 1992. *CRESST performance assessment models: Assessing content area explanations.* Los Angeles, Calif.: National Center for Research on Evaluation, Standards, and Student Testing (CRESST), UCLA.

Baron, J.B. 1991. Strategies for the development of effective performance exercises. *Applied Measurement in Education* 4: 305-318.

Baron, J B., and B. Kallick. 1985. Assessing thinking: What are we looking for? And how can we find it? In *Developing minds: A resource book for teaching thinking,* ed. A. Costa. Alexandria, Va.: Association for Supervision and Curriculum Development.

Berk, R A. 1986a. Minimum competency testing: Status and potential. In *The future of testing,* ed. B S. Plate and J C. Witts, 88-144. Hillsdale, N.J.: Lawrence Erlbaum Associates.

Berk, R A., ed. 1986b. *Performance assessment: Methods and applications.* Baltimore, Md.: The Johns Hopkins University Press.

Berliner, D. 1984. The executive functions of teaching. *The Instructor* 93(2): 28-40.

Berliner, D C. 1979. Tempus educare, In *Research on teaching*, ed. P L. Peterson and H.J. Walberg. Berkeley, Calif.: McCutchan.

Bond, L., L. Friedman, and A. van der Ploeg. 1994. *Surveying the landscape of state educational assessment programs*. Washington, D.C.: Council for Educational Development and Research and the National Education Association.

Brennan, R.L. 1983. *Elements of generalization theory*. Iowa City, Iowa: American College Testing Program.

Brookhart, S.M. 1993. Teacher's grading practices: meaning and values. *Journal of Educational Measurement* 30(2): 123-142.

Calkins, L.M. 1986. *The art of teaching writing*. Portsmouth, N.H.: Heinemann.

Cannell, J.J. 1988. Nationally normed elementary achievement testing in America's public schools: How all 50 states are above the national average. *Educational Measurement: Issues and Practices* 7(2): 5-9.

Carnevale, A.P., L.J. Gainer, and A.S. Meltzer. 1990. *Workplace basics: The essential skills employers want*. San Francisco: Jossey-Bass.

Cazden, C.B. 1986. Classroom discourse. In *Handbook of research on teaching*, 3d ed. M. C. Wittrock. New York: Macmillan.

Coleman, J.S. 1972. The evaluation of equality of educational opportunity. In *On equality of educational opportunity*, ed. F. Mosteller and D.P. Moynihan. New York: Vintage Books.

College Board. 1983. *Academic preparation for college: What students need to know and be able to do*. New York: College Entrance Examination Board.

Conley, D.T. 1996. Assessment. In *A handbook for student performance assessment in an era of restructuring*, ed. R.E. Blum and J.A. Arter. Alexandria, Va.: Association for Supervision and Curriculum Development.

Costa, A. 1984. Mediating the metacognitive. *Educational Leadership* 42: 57-62.

Countryman, L.L., and M. Schroeder. 1996. When students lead parent-teacher conferences. *Educational Leadership* 53(7): 64-68.

Darling-Hammond. L., and J. Ancess. 1994. *Graduation by portfolio at Central Park East Secondary School*. New York: National Center for Restructuring Education, Schools, and Teaching, Columbia University.

Darling-Hammond, L., J. Ancess, and B. Falk. 1995. *Authentic assessment in action: Studies of schools and student work*. New York: Teacher's College Press.

Dewey, J. 1916. *Democracy and education*. New York: Macmillan.

Dossey, J.A., I.V.S. Mullis, and C.O. Jones. 1993. *Can students do mathematical problem solving?* Washington, D.C.: U.S. Department of Education, Office of Educational Research and Improvement.

Doyle, W. 1992. Curriculum and pedagogy. In *Handbook of research in curriculum*, ed. P.W. Jackson. New York: Macmillan.

Durm, M.W. 1993. An A is not an A: A history of grading. *The Educational Forum* 57: 294-297.

Durst, R.K., and G.E. Newell. 1989. The uses of function: James Britton's category system and research on writing. *Review of Educational Research* 59(4): 375-394.

Farkas, F., W. Friedman, J. Boese, and G. Shaw. 1994. *First things first: What Americans expect from public schools*. New York: Public Agenda.

Feldt, L.S., and R.L. Brennan. 1993. Reliability. In *Educational measurement*, 3d ed. R.L. Linn. Phoenix, Ariz.: Onyx Press.

Finn, C.E., Jr. 1990. The biggest reform of all. *Phi Delta Kappan* 7(8): 584-592.

Fisher, C.W., D.C. Berliner, N. Filby, R.S. Marliave, L.S. Cahen, and M.M. Dishaw. 1980. Teaching behaviors, academic learning time and student achievement: An overview. In *Time to learn*, ed. C. Denham and A. Lieberman. Washington, D.C.: National Institute of Education.

Fitts, P.M. 1964. Perceptual-motor skill learning. In *Categories of human learning*, ed. A.W. Melton. New York: Wiley.

Fitts, P.M., and M.I. Posner. 1967. *Human performance*. Belmont, Calif.: Brooks Cole.

Fitzpatrick, K.A., M. Kulieke, J. Hillary, and V. Begitschke. 1996. The instructional resource network: Supporting the alignment of curriculum instruction and assessment. In *A handbook for student performance assessment in an era of restructuring*, ed. R.E. Blum and J.A. Arter. Alexandria, Va.: Association for Supervision and Curriculum Development.

Florida Department of State. 1996. *Science: Pre K-12 sunshine state standards and instructional practices*. Tallahassee, Fla.: Author.

Frederiksen, C.H. 1977. Semantic processing units in understanding text. In *Discourse production and comprehension*, ed. R.O. Freedle. Norwood, N.J.: Ablex.

Frederiksen, J.R., and A. Collins. 1989. A systems approach to educational testing. *Educational Researcher* 18(9): 27-32.

Futrell, M.H. 1987. A message long overdue. *Education Week* 7(14): 9.

Gandal, M. 1997. *Making standards matter, 1997: An annual fifty-state report on efforts to raise academic standards*. Washington, D.C.: American Federation of Teachers.

Glaser, R., and R. Linn. 1993. Foreword to *Setting performance standards for student achievement*. L. Shepard. Stanford, Calif.: National Academy of Education, Stanford University.

Glickman, C. 1993. *Reviewing America's schools*. San Francisco: Jossey-Bass.

Goodman, Y.M. 1978. Kid watching: An alternative to testing. *National Elementary School Principal* 57: 41-45.

Guskey, T.R., ed. 1996a. *ASCD yearbook, 1996: Communicating student learning*. Alexandria, Va.: Association for Supervision and Curriculum Development.

———. 1996b. Reporting on student learning: Lessons from the past: prescriptions for the future. *ASCD yearbook, 1996: Communicating student learning*. Alexandria, Va.: Association for Supervision and Curriculum Development.

Hampel, R.L. 1986. *The last little citadel*. Boston: Houghton-Mifflin.

Hansen. J. 1987. *When writers read*. Portsmouth, N.H.: Heinemann.

———. J. 1994. Literacy portfolios: Windows on potential. In *Authentic reading assessment: Practices and possibilities*, ed. S.W. Valencia, E.H. Hiebert, and P.P. Afflerrbach. Newark, Del.: International Reading Association.

Hawkins, D. 1973. I, thou, it: The triangular relationship. In *The open classroom reader*, ed. C. Silberman. New York: Random House.

Herman, J. 1996. Technical quality matters. In *A handbook for student performance assessment in an era of restructuring*, ed. R.E. Blum and J.A. Arter. Alexandria, Va.: Association for Supervision and Curriculum Development.

Hirsch, E.D., Jr. 1987. *Cultural literacy: What every American needs to know*. Boston: Houghton-Mifflin.

———. 1997. *The schools we need: Why we don't have them*. New York: Doubleday.

Knight, P. 1992. How I use portfolios in mathematics. *Educational Leadership* 49(8): 71-72.

Lane, S., M. Liu, R.D. Ankenmann, and C.A. Stone. 1996. Generalizability and validity of a mathematics performance assessment. *Journal of Educational Measurement* 33(1): 71-92.

Linn, R. 1994. Performance assessment: Policy promises and technical measurement standards. *Educational Researcher* 23(9): 4-14.

Linn, R.L., and N.E. Gronlund. 1995. *Measurement and assessment in teaching*, 7th ed. Englewood Cliffs, N.J.: Prentice-Hall.

Marzano, R.J. 1990. Standardized tests: Do they measure general cognitive abilities? *NASSP Bulletin* 74(526): 93-101.

———. 1992. *A different kind of classroom: Teaching with dimensions of learning*. Alexandria, Va.: Association for Supervision and Curriculum Development.

Marzano, R.J., and A.L. Costa. 1988. Question: Do standardized tests measure cognitive skills? Answer: No. *Educational Leadership* 45(8): 66-73.

Marzano. R.J., and J.S. Kendall. 1992. Unpublished data. Aurora, Co.: Mid-continent Regional Educational Laboratory.

——. 1996. *A comprehensive guide to designing standards-based districts, schools, and classrooms*. Alexandria, Va.: Association for Supervision and Curriculum Development.

Marzano, R.J., D.J. Pickering, D.E. Arredondo, G.J. Blackburn, R.S. Brandt, and C.A. Moffett. 1992. *Dimensions of learning: Teacher's manual*. Alexandria, Va.: Association for Supervision and Curriculum Development.

Marzano, R.J., D.J. Pickering, and J. McTighe. 1993. *Assessing student outcomes*. Alexandria, Va.: Association for Supervision and Curriculum Development.

McDonald, J.P., S. Smith, D. Turner, M. Finney, and E. Barton. 1993. *Graduation by exhibition: Assessing genuine achievement*. Alexandria, Va.: Association for Supervision and Curriculum.

McREL Institute. 1994. *A summary report of studies of the effectiveness of standards-based education in the Aurora Public Schools*. Aurora, Colo.: Author.

McTighe, J., and S. Ferrara. 1996. Performance-based assessment in the classroom: A planning framework. In *A handbook for student performance assessment in an era of restructuring*, ed. R.E. Blum and J.A. Arter. Alexandria, Va.: Association for Supervision and Curriculum Development.

Meyer, C.A. 1992. What's the difference between authentic and performance assessment? *Educational Leadership* 49(8): 39-40.

Mitchell, R. 1992. *Testing for learning: How new approaches to evaluation can improve American schools*. New York: The Free Press.

Mitchell, R., and M. Neill. 1992. *Criteria for evaluation of student assessment*. Washington, D.C.: National Forum On Assessment.

Mullis, I.V.S., E.H. Owen, and G.W. Phillips. 1990. *America's challenge: Accelerating academic achievement (A summary of findings from 20 years of NAEP)*. Princeton, N.J.: Educational Testing Service.

National Assessment of Educational Progress. 1992. *Framework for the 1994 national assessment of educational progress mathematics assessment*. Washington, D.C.: Author.

National Commission on Excellence in Education. 1983. *A nation at risk: The imperative for educational reform*. Washington, D.C.: Government Printing Office.

National Council of Teachers of Mathematics. 1989. *Curriculum and evaluation standards for school mathematics*. Reston, Va.: Author.

National Education Goals Panel. 1991. *The national education goals report: Building a nation of learners*. Washington, D.C.: Author.

National Governors Association. 1996. *1996 National education summit policy statement*. Washington, D.C.: Author.

National Science Board Commission on Precollege Education in Mathematics, Science and Technology. 1983. *Educating Americans for the 21st century.* Washington, D.C.: National Science Board Commission.

Neill, Monty, and others. 1997. *Testing our children: A report card on state assessment systems.* Cambridge, Ma.: National Center for Fair and Open Testing (Fairtest).

Newell, A., and H.A. Simon. 1972. *Human problem solving.* Englewood Cliffs, N.J.: Prentice-Hall.

Newmann, F.M., W.G. Secado, and G.G. Wehlage. 1995. *A guide to authentic instruction and assessment: Vision, standards and scoring.* Madison, Wisc.: Wisconsin Center for Educational Research, University of Wisconsin.

Norman, D. 1969. *Memory and attention.* New York: John Wiley & Sons.

O'Donnell, A., and A.E. Woolfolk. 1991. *Elementary and secondary teachers' beliefs about testing and grading.* Paper presented at the annual meeting of the American Psychological Association, San Francisco.

Olson, L. 1995a. Standards times 50, struggling for standards: An Education Week special report. *Education Week* (April 12): 14-22.

———. 1995b. Cards on the table. *Education Week* (June 14): 23-28.

Ornstein, A.C. 1994. Grading practices and policies: An overview and some suggestions. *NASSP Bulletin* 78(561): 55-64.

Payne, D.A. 1974. *The assessment of learning.* Lexington, Mass.: Heath.

Perkins, D.N. 1992. *Smart schools: From training memories to educating minds.* New York: The Free Press.

Powell, A.G., E. Farrar, and D.K. Cohen. 1985. *The shopping mall high school.* Boston: Houghton-Mifflin.

Quellmalz, E.S. 1987. Developing reasoning skills. In *Teaching thinking skills: Theory and practice*, ed. J.B. Baron and R.J. Sternberg. New York: W.H. Freeman.

Reckase, M.D. 1995. Portfolio assessment: A theoretical estimate of score reliability. *Educational Measurement: Issues and Practices* 14(1):12-14, 31.

Resnick, L.B. 1987a. Learning in school and out. *Educational Researcher* 16(9): 13-20.

———. 1987b. *Education and learning to think.* Washington, D.C.: National Academy Press.

Resnick, L.B., and D.P. Resnick. 1992. Assessing the thinking curriculum: New tools for educational reform. In *Changing assessments: Alternative views of aptitude, achievement and instruction*, ed. B.R. Gifford and M.C. O'Conor. Boston: Kluwer Academic Press.

Rowe, H. 1985. *Problem solving and intelligence.* Hillsdale, N.J.: Lawrence Erlbaum Associates.

Secretary's Commission on Achieving Necessary Skills (SCANS). 1991. *What work requires of schools: A SCANS report for America 2000.* Washington, D.C.: U.S. Department of Labor.

Shavelson, R.J., and G.P. Baxter. What we've learned about assessing hands-on science. *Educational Leadership* 49(8): 21-25.

Shavelson, R.J., and N.M. Webb. 1993. *Generalizability theory: A primer.* Newbury Park, Calif.: Sage Publishing.

Shavelson, R.J., X. Gao, and G.R. Baxter. 1993. *Sampling variability of performance assessments* (CSE Tech. Rep. No. 361). Santa Barbara, Calif.: National Center for Research in Evaluation, Standards and Student Testing, UCLA.

Shavelson, R.J., N.M. Webb, and G. Rowley. 1989. Generalizability theory. *American Psychologist* 44: 922-932.

Shepard, L. 1989. Why we need better assessments. *Educational Leadership* 46(7): 41-47.

———. 1993. *Setting performance standards for student achievement.* Stanford, Calif.: National Academy of Education, Stanford University.

Sizer, T. 1985. *Horace's compromise.* Boston: Houghton-Mifflin.

Spady, W.G. 1988. Organizing for results: The basis of authentic restructuring and reform. *Educational Leadership* 46(2): 4-8.

———. 1995. Outcome-based education: From instructional reform to paradigm restructuring. In *School improvement programs,* ed. J.H. Block, S.T. Everson, and T.R. Guskey. New York: Scholastic.

Sperling, D. 1996. Collaborative assessment: Making high standards a reality for all students. In *A handbook for student performance assessment in an era of restrucuturing,* ed. R.E. Blum and J.A. Arter. Alexandria, Va.: Association for Supervision and Curriculum Development.

Staton, J. 1980. Writing and counseling: Using a dialogue journal. *Language Arts* 57: 514-518.

Stevenson, H.W., and J.W. Stigler. 1992. *The learning gap: Why our schools are failing and what we can learn from Japanese and Chinese education.* New York: Touchstone.

Stiggins, R.J. 1994. *Student-centered classroom assessment.* New York: Merrill.

Stodolsky, S.S. 1989. Is teaching really by the book? In *Eighty-ninth yearbook of the National Society for the Study of Education,* ed. P.W. Jackson and S. Haroutunian-Gordon. Chicago: University of Chicago Press.

Thaiss, C. 1986. *Language across the curriculum in the elementary grades.* Urbana, Ill.: ERIC Clearinghouse on Reading and Communication Skills and National Council of Teachers of English.

Uchida, D., M. Cetron, and F. McKenzie. 1996. *Preparing students for the 21st century*. Reston, Va.: American Association of School Administrators.

Valencia, S. 1987. *Novel formats for assessing prior knowledge and measures of reading comprehension*. Paper presented at the annual meeting of the American Educational Research Association, Washington, D.C.

van Dijk. T.A. 1980. *Macrostructures*. Hillsdale, N.J.: Lawrence Erlbaum Associates.

The Wall Street Journal. 1997. If you have brains, you might decide to skip this test. (March 28).

Wiggins, G. 1989. Teaching to the (authentic) task. *Educational Leadership* 46(7): 41-47.

———. 1991. Standards, not standardization: Evoking quality student work. *Educational Leadership* 48(5): 18-25.

———. 1993a. Assessment, authenticity, context and validity. *Phi Delta Kappan*: 200-214.

———. 1993b. *Assessing student performances: Exploring the purpose and limits of testing*. San Francisco: Jossey-Bass.

———. Toward better report cards. *Educational Leadership*. 52(2): 28-37.

Wilde, S. 1996. *Notes from a kid watcher: Selected writings of Yetta M. Goodman*. Portsmouth, N.H.: Heinemann.

Willis, S. 1996. Student exhibitions put higher-order skills to the test. *Education Update* 38(2): 1-3.

Winograd, P., and F.D. Perkins. 1996. Authentic assessment in the classroom: Principles and practices. In *A handbook for student performance assessment in an era of restructuring*, ed. R.E. Blum and J.A. Arter. Alexandria, Va.: Association for Supervision and Curriculum Development.

Yoon, B., L. Burstein, and K. Gold. (n.d.) *Assessing the content validity of teachers' reports of content coverage and its relationship to student achievement*. Los Angeles: Center for Research in Evaluation, Standards and Student Testing, UCLA.

Young, A., and T. Fulwiler, ed. 1986. *Writing across the disciplines*. Portsmouth, N.H.: Heinemann.